I0411854

Ethics, Counterinsurgency, And Perceptions,
In The Information Era
by

School of Advanced Military Studies
United States Army Command and General Staff College
Fort Leavenworth, Kansas

Abstract

ETHICS, COUNTERINSURGENCY, AND PERCEPTIONS IN THE INFORMATION ERA by
MAJ Steven Basilici, United States Army, 72 pages.

From antiquity to the present there has been cultural tension over different views of what
is right and what is wrong, and every culture desires to apply their values universally to the rest of
the world. When a nation chooses to go to war and exercises its sovereign right to use military
force, it must act in a way that is ethically acceptable and morally justifiable in the eyes of its
people. When one is perceived to act ethically one is acting in accordance with the perceiver's
values. Defining what these values are and determining, in the broader sense, whether they are
right or wrong is not the issue of this paper. The central issue of this paper is analyzing the
affects caused by the perception that actions do not support stated values when that perception is
created in the information environment. No country in the world today can act autonomously;
each must justify its actions or inevitably face failure. Especially challenged is the country that
justifies its choice to go to war based upon universally stated values and then in the conduct of
that war consistently act in ways that do not support those values.

The thesis of this study is that when physical actions that are not consistent with a
nation's stated values are introduced into the information environment, they can be strategically
adverse to that nation. Stated another way, in the present Information Era, it is very difficult for a
government, especially a foreign, democratic government, to win a counterinsurgent war when
the actions of their soldiers do not consistently support stated values. What is the importance of
the relationship between ethics and counterinsurgency? In a single word, the answer is
perception. The case of a Western, democratic government conducting a counterinsurgency in a
foreign country is perhaps the best scenario with which to test this thesis, because of the stated
Western values of freedom of speech and human rights. However, this thesis does not just apply
to counterinsurgent warfare. This thesis is applicable to all forms of warfare conducted in the
present age and for the foreseeable future. Through an analysis of the relationships among ethics,
counterinsurgency, and how perceptions are created in the information environment, the
enhanced dynamics affecting the conduct of warfare in the 21st century will be better understood.
Through this study, weaknesses in industrial-era military doctrine will become more evident, and
military, joint, and inter-agency transformation can be improved.

TABLE OF CONTENTS

TABLE OF FIGURES

INTRODUCTION: Ethics, Counterinsurgency, and Perceptions in the Information Era

> Theory becomes infinitely more difficult as soon as it touches the realm of moral values.
>
> Carl Von Clausewitz[1]

From the ancient era of warfare onward there has always been the necessity for governments and their armies to justify their reasons for going to war, and during the conduct of war act in accordance with accepted values. From Biblical times to the invasion of Iraq by coalition forces led by the United States in 2003, actions have been driven by values and necessity. In chapter nine of the first book of the Bible (1450-1440 BC), God speaks to Noah and establishes the sanctity of human life and the consequences for anyone who should violate it: "Whoso sheddeth man's blood, by man shall his blood be shed: for in the image of God made he man."[2] This verse establishes one of the foundational purposes of many future governments as protector of the governed. In this single verse one finds the prohibition against the taking of human life- the protection of people; the consequences for violating this prohibition- the death sentence and by extension a government's authority in executing that sentence; and the purpose for both- the fact that man is made in God's image. Consistent with this earlier precept, later in the Bible God directs the Israelites to completely destroy the nations of the Hittites, Amorites, Canaanites, Perizzites, Hivites, and Jebusites[3] as abominations before God, because their "sons and daughters they have burnt in the fire to their gods."[4] These nations customarily made human sacrifices to their gods and in doing so the Bible records that these actions brought condemnation down upon them through the warfare waged upon them by Israel.

---

[1]Carl Von Clausewitz, *On War* (Princeton: Princeton University Press, 1984), 136.
[2]Genesis 9:6 KJV (King James Version).
[3]Deut. 20:17 KJV.
[4]Deut. 12:31 KJV.

Essentially the same argument about the sanctify of human life is made over three

millennia later by the Founding Fathers of the United States in the *Declaration of Independence*

where they argued, "We hold these truths to be self-evident, that all men are created equal, that

they are endowed by their Creator with certain unalienable Rights, that among these are Life,

Liberty, and the pursuit of Happiness."[5] The Founding Fathers justified their collective act of

revolution by appealing to a Divine authority based upon the "Law of Nature and of Nature's

God"[6] over a human authority. They believed their actions were justifiable based upon accepted

Judeo-Christian ethic as laid down in the Bible and applied to government through the work of

key thinkers such as Samuel B. Rutherford (1600-1661) in his work *Lex Rex* (Law is King), and

John Locke (1632-1704).[7] Through both Biblical and American Revolution examples one can

clearly see the relationship between values and actions being played out. In the case of the

American Revolution, once the Declaration of Independence was signed and presented to the

King of England, the first thing the Founders did was field a regular European-style army. Why

did they do this? They understood that their actions had to match their stated values; in order for

the Revolution to be seen as honorable and legitimate, they had to act according to the accepted

laws of war and be prepared to meet the British in the field. Later, as commander of the

Continental Army, Washington's General Orders of Conduct reflect this understanding. Part of

his General Orders to the newly formed American army, issued in Fredericksburg 1778, stated

that,

> Purity of morals being the only sure foundation of public happiness in any country, and
> highly conducive to order, subordination, and success in an army, it will be well worthy

---

[5] *The Declaration of Independence of the United States of America* (Philadelphia: John Dunlap, 1776).

[6] *Declaration of Independence*, Introduction.

[7] Francis Schaeffer, *How Shall We Then Live? The Rise and Decline of Western Thought and Culture* (Wheaton, IL: Crossway Books, 1976), 108-110.

the emulation of officers of every rank and class to encourage it both by the influence of example and the penalties of authority.[8]

General Washington believed that moral purity formed the foundation for one of our nation's stated values, namely the pursuit of happiness. He also understood that it was through the articulation and enforcement of the 'purity of morals' in support of this value that would dictate the behavior of his soldiers during time of war. General George Washington believed that if he wanted to maintain the legitimacy of a professional army such orders were essential and that once given they had to be enforced; the actions of his men had to support and reinforce the nation's stated values. A disconnect in actions and values, especially in a soldier of the Continental Army, would have hurt the cause of the war and compromised America's independence. The absolute language of binding documents, such as the Bible, the Declaration of Independence, and the Constitution, is still with us today and underpins the foreign policy of the United States. The first paragraph of the first page of the National Security Strategy of the United States of America, 2002, states that

> People everywhere want to be able to speak freely; choose who will govern them; worship as they please; educate their children – male and female; own property; and enjoy the benefits of their labor. *These values of freedom are right and true for every person, in every society* – and the duty of protecting these values against their enemies is *the common calling of freedom-loving people across the globe and across the ages* (emphasis added by author).[9]

As one thinks about the dominant influence the United States enjoys today as the world superpower, one might express the opinion that the US is somewhat arrogant in its assertions. But, the preamble, and Articles I and II of the Universal Declaration of Human Rights, signed on 10 December 1948 and translated into over 300 languages, state much the same. "The equal and inalienable rights of all members of the human family are the foundation of freedom, justice and

---

[8]George Washington, *General Orders* (Fredericksburg: 1778).
[9]*The National Security Strategy of the United States of America* (Washington: The White House, 2002), 1.

peace in the world."[10] Article II contains the most striking, all-encompassing language within the document stating that,

> Everyone is entitled to all the rights and freedoms set forth in this Declaration, **without distinction of any kind**, such as race, colour, sex, language, religion, political or other opinion, national or social origin, property, birth or other status. Furthermore, **no distinction shall be made on the basis of the political, jurisdictional or international status** of the country or territory to which a person belongs, whether it be independent, trust, non-self-governing or under any other limitation of sovereignty (emphasis added by author).[11]

From antiquity to the present there has been cultural tension over different views of what is right and what is wrong, and almost all cultures desire to apply their values universally to the rest of the world. When a nation chooses to go to war and exercises its sovereign right to use military force, it must act in a way that is ethically acceptable and morally justifiable in the eyes of its people. When one is perceived to act ethically one is acting in accordance with the perceiver's values. Defining what these values are and determining, in the broader sense, whether they are right or wrong is not the issue of this paper. The central issue of this paper is analyzing the affects caused by the perception that actions do not support stated values when that perception is created in the information environment. No country in the world today can act autonomously; each must justify its actions or inevitably face failure. Especially challenged is the country that justifies its choice to go to war based upon universally stated values and then in the conduct of that war consistently acts in ways that do not support those values.

The thesis of this study is that when physical actions that are not consistent with a government's stated values are introduced into the information environment, they can be strategically adverse to the counterinsurgent. Stated another way, in the present information age,

---

[10]Universal Declaration of Human Rights, *Preamble* [document online]; available from http://www.unhchr.ch/udhr/lang/eng.pdf, Internet, accessed 18 January 2006. This PDF version of the Universal Declaration of Human Rights is an English translation of the declaration adopted by the United Nations on 10 December 1948.

[11]Universal Declaration of Human Rights, *Article I.*

the age of globalization, it is very difficult for a government, especially a foreign, democratic government, to win a counterinsurgent war when the physical actions of their soldiers do not consistently support stated values. What is the importance of the relationship between ethics and counterinsurgency? In a single word, the answer is *perception*. If in counterinsurgency "the military objective generally seeks to obtain the willing acceptance of a lawfully constituted agency, group, or government by the population in the AO"[12] (area of operations), then the linkage between actions (as ethical or unethical), stated values, and perception, becomes the most critical relationship to understand and manage. To a lesser degree the proper management of action to value perceptions is also true for the insurgent. For both parties, actions taken during the conduct of the struggle must reflect the stated values of each, because ultimately insurgent warfare is a war of political will. Therefore, the stated purpose for waging war by the government of the counterinsurgent must reflect the values of its people and must be mirrored in the way in which its agents, including the military, conduct the counterinsurgency. Legitimacy is the overarching strategic objective of counterinsurgency and must be maintained through ethical conduct that produces the perception that the counterinsurgent force is "acting under the authority and in the interest of"[13] the population for which it is contending. The case of a Western, democratic government conducting a counterinsurgency in a foreign country is perhaps the best scenario with which to test this hypothesis because of the stated Western values of freedom of speech and human rights. However, this thesis does not just apply to counterinsurgent warfare. This thesis is applicable to both conventional and unconventional warfare conducted in the present age and for the foreseeable future. Through an analysis of the relationships among ethics, counterinsurgency, and how perceptions are created in the information environment, the enhanced dynamics affecting the conduct of warfare in the 21st century will be better understood.

---

[12]Department of the Army, *FM 3-07, Stability Operations and Support Operations* (Washington, DC: Department of the Army, 2003). 1-19.

Weaknesses in industrial-era military doctrine will become more evident, and military, joint, and inter-agency transformation can be improved.

This monograph comprises five chapters following the introduction. Chapter one is an historical overview from the Ancient to the beginning of the Industrial Era of Warfare that focuses on the relationship between the people, government, and army as portrayed by the Clausewitzian Trinity. The purpose of this overview is to show that while the people's perception of ethical conduct in the prosecution of war has always been a component of the nature of war, up until the Information Age, it has not been considered decisive. Chapter two will continue the historical overview with the Industrial Era by analyzing the significant geopolitical effects of nationalism and the technological advances in communications on the conduct of war.

Chapter three will encompass the main argument of this monograph as a theory on the dynamics of war for the 21st century. In this chapter the technological advances of the information age, the power of globalization on free-market enterprise, and universally acknowledged values are shown to converge in the information environment and superempower people as the decisive component in the nature of war for the 21st century. Of key importance will be the argument that the speed and diffusion of information and its effect on global or regional perception has become a crucial line of operation for governments and their militaries in the ethical conduct of warfare because there has occurred an "equalization of power" between state and non-state opponents. It is this equalization of power that has made information a competitive line of operation.

Chapter four will analyze four information events that occurred during the Industrial and Information Eras of Warfare in order to show a contrast between the two. The purpose of the analysis is to show the evolutionary changes in information flow and their affects on the strategic,

---

[13]FM 3-07, 1-19.

operational, and tactical levels of war. A background is given for each event followed by an analysis from an action to values point of view to determine if a perception of disconnect occurred between those actions and the stated values of the government involved. Finally, a contrast between corrective actions taken on the part of the government or military involved will be assessed to show long term ramifications on military operations at the strategic, operational, and tactical levels.

Chapter five shows the way ahead with concluding remarks and recommendations for what must be done in order to more fully understand and harness the emergent dynamics of the speed and diffusion of information for operational planning. Through this endeavor, a heightened awareness of these extremely powerful dynamics will enable planners, and especially the warrior on the ground, to more effectively fight our nation's wars in the 21st century and foreseeable future.

CHAPTER 1: From the Bible to the Treaty of Westphalia

The purpose of this chapter is to show that the military to military (mil to mil) relationship has dominated the nature of warfare throughout recorded human history from Biblical times to the ascendancy of the nation state. During this same period information flow was limited, primarily affecting the linkage between the government and army rather than the people. In explaining this, the theory that war is a manifestation of the relationship among the people of a nation, the military of that nation, and the government; a construct known as the Clausewitzian Trinity, has been adopted. The Clausewitzian Trinity represents a timeless model for the visual depiction of the nature of war while allowing for the application of different forms of war; i.e., conventional versus unconventional warfare. Figure 1 shows a simplistic understanding of how one may apply the model to both forms of warfare in regard to strategic priorities. As the model depicts, conventional warfare begins with a military versus military priority with emphasis on destruction of an enemy's army, leading to the capitulation of the government, and the control of the people. Conversely, in unconventional and counterinsurgent warfare, the people, as a population, become the military target of both the insurgent and counterinsurgent force with the struggle for dominance ultimately achieved through winning legitimacy in the eyes of the people. If enough of the people are won over to the insurgent or revolutionary cause, as was the case in the French Revolution, then the army of the government will ultimately be defeated or co-opted by the revolutionary force, followed by the capitulation and replacement of the government. On the other hand, if the government or counterinsurgent maintains its position of authority through actions that sustain and increase the popular perception of the government's legitimacy, then the insurgent will be defeated.

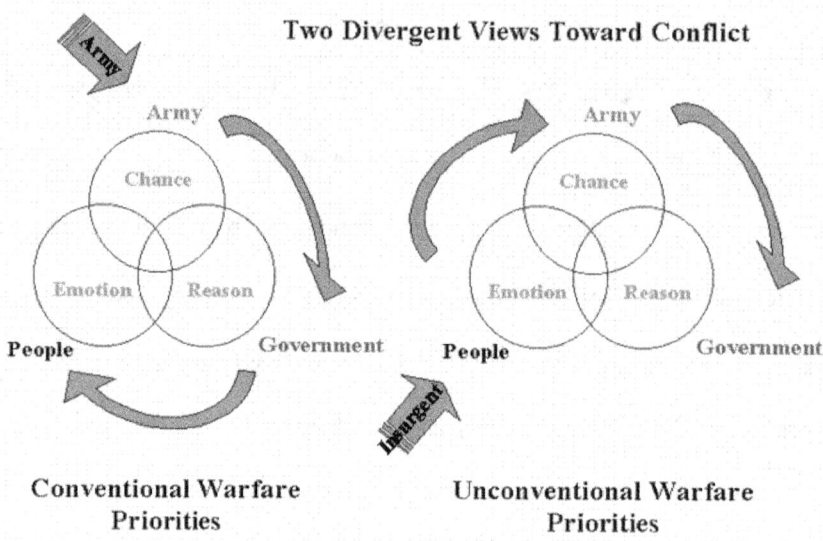

Figure 1. The Clausewitzian Trinity and Two Divergent Views Toward Conflict[14]

While it may be easy to identify the strategic priorities of different forms of war using this paradigm, the thing that makes it timeless is its duality, that is, the dual nature of Clausewitz' conception as understood in what is termed in this study as the human-factor trinity. The human-factor trinity comprises reason, chance, and passion and transparently co-exists along with the government, army, and people respectively. Clausewitz' writings on the nature of war are relevant today because he perceived that both a physical and non-physical dimension to life exists and had to be structurally incorporated into an understanding of the nature of warfare. Just as "war is…a true political instrument, a continuation of political intercourse, carried on with other means,"[15] both war and politics must be both an extension and expression of the people.

This thought in itself is no great leap; others have touched upon the metaphysical or teleological aspect of human nature in warfare. For example Machiavelli called it *virtue* and

---

[14]Steven Basilici and J. Simmons, *Transformation, A Bold Case for Unconventional Warfare* (Monterey: Naval Postgraduate School, 2004), 24.
[15]Carl Von Clausewitz, 87.

Fortuna, but Clausewitz was the first to assign teleological words to each of the components of a model he developed. The important distinction is that these words connote things that are non-physical, things that are unknowable through empirical evidence: reason, chance, and passion. It is on this point that Clausewitz departs from Jomini, Machiavelli, and Frederick the Great. Clausewitz refers to the unknowable elsewhere as the fog and friction of war. When two armies are facing each other on the battlefield this aspect of the Clausewitzian trinity is less important, but when control of the people as a population is the specific military object, as in counterinsurgency, 'passion' as it relates to the popular will of the people becomes a dominant aspect. "As Aristotle wrote in support of teleology, 'Nature adapts the organ to the function, and not the function to the organ.'"[16] In the same way, Clausewitz understood that human nature as it is expressed in societies (reason, chance, and passion) adapts to the manifestation of warfare, not the other way around: the manifestation of warfare, or any other manifestation, is not what forms human nature. In other words, warfare is only one of many social manifestations and all societal manifestations are expressions of a mixture of both the physical world and the non-physical aspects of human nature. In Clausewitz' own words: "Military activity is never directed against material force alone; it is always aimed simultaneously at the moral forces which give it life, and the two cannot be separated."[17]

Examples of warrior cultures in history are commonplace, such as the Spartans of ancient Greece up to the end of the Peloponnesian War and the Japanese up to the end of World War II, but it would be a stretch to argue that these people existed solely in order to conduct warfare or were made a society by the power of warfare acting upon them. Rather, as societies they chose to be war-like in order to survive and dominate their world. These are important distinctions when

---

[16]Wikipedia, *Teleology* [document online]; available from http://en.wikipedia.org/ , Internet, accessed on January 9, 2006, this quote is taken from Aristotle's De partib., animal., IV, xii, 694b; 13.
[17]Carl Von Clausewitz, 137.

one considers a non-physical thing, such as information, and the physical affect it can put in motion through individuals to the collective groups of people that make up societal entities.

Keeping the Clausewitzian Trinity in mind, the fact that warfare has been dominated by its conventional mil to mil form is readily evident through an overview of history. This is not to say that the 'people' were any less of an essential component within Clausewitz' paradigm, but that as populations they have been treated differently. By and large populations were not seen as the priority or focus of the war-fighting; their army was. From the Biblical record, through early Greek and Roman history, and in Western Civilization up to World War II, populations were much more victims of circumstance. In conducting this historical overview, a periodic or era view of warfare is adopted. These eras include the Ancient, Medieval, Gunpowder, Industrial, and Information Eras of Warfare.[18] A further grouping is made based upon the relative affects of information on the history of war collectively. To this end the Ancient, Medieval and Gunpowder Eras of Warfare will be dealt with in one section, the Industrial Era in a second section, and the Information Era of warfare in a third section.

The Ancient Era of War

In analyzing the Ancient, Medieval, and Gunpowder Eras of War, three main points are emphasized: that the decisive component of warfare was primarily the military, how populations were dealt with, and how information flow and perceptions affected the overall conduct of war. Figure 2 depicts a snapshot of how the Clausewitzian Trinity applies to these first three eras.

---

[18]Wikipedia, *History of Warfare* [document online]; available from http://en.wikipedia.org/ Internet, accessed on January 9, 2006.

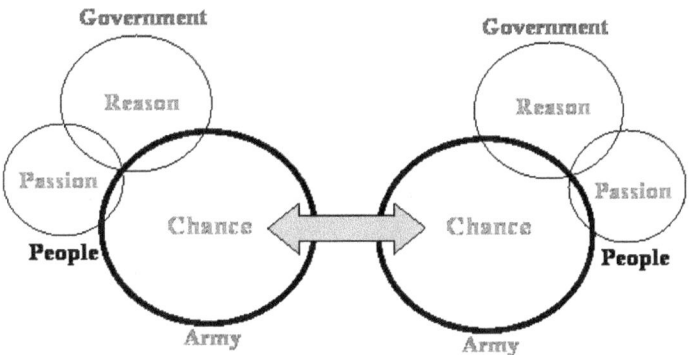

Figure 2. The Decisive Component in War from the Ancient to the Gunpowder Era

The sizes of the circles in Figure 2 represent the dominance or importance of each of the components in regard to decisiveness in the conduct and outcome of warfare. The people were least important; the government or sovereign were next, leaving the army as the most decisive. Although this may seem simplistic, it does give one a solid comprehensive picture of the nature of war that can be evaluated through historical analysis. An excellent example of the interrelatedness of these three components in the ancient era can be seen in Sun Tzu's writings from the fourth century BC. Sun Tzu was asked by Ho-lü, King of Wu, if he was a good enough commander to organize and drill women in military formation. Sun Tzu replied that he could and formed one hundred and eighty of the king's concubines into two company formations choosing the king's favorite two concubines as the company commanders. After instructing the ladies, Sun Tzu gave the orders to begin drilling them only to receive laughter from his new female recruits. After two attempts with the same results, he gave orders to have the two favorite concubines beheaded. When the king objected, Sun Tzu replied that "Your servant has already received your appointment as commander and when the commander is at the head of the army he need not accept all the sovereign's orders."[19] Sun Tzu then executed the two favored concubines, replaced

them, and drilled the companies without further problems. Afterwards, when the King refused to

come and inspect the troops, Sun Tzu said, "The King likes only empty words. He is not capable

of putting them into practice."[20] Through the interaction between sovereign and military

commander, one can see the dominance of what was considered a good military commander once

he has been given his mandate. Sun Tzu and the king, who subsequently promoted him to

general of his army, understood that for the king to be able to wield his sovereign authority, he

needed exceptional commanders and men in arms to do so. The lives of people in the Ancient

Era of Warfare were expendable compared to the strong emphasis put on the safety of each

soldier and person today. "When the general beheaded the favored concubines in view of the

other concubines he was engaging 'the people' and emotion directly – separating their allegiance

from the king unto himself. Sun Tzu's method was consistent with the values of the time and

succeeded."[21] Interestingly, this same tactic has been used by guerrillas and terrorist

organizations through the ages to ensure allegiance within their organizations. Finally, to the

contemporary mind, in the case of the two favored concubines, here representing people, their

lives were held cheaply and they were killed simply to make a point. These tactics would hardly

be acceptable in today's modern state system.

While history shows that the mil to mil relationship was by and large the decisive

component in warfare, one can also identify the government's role and the necessity for their

armies to act in accordance with accepted values. As stated earlier, actions have been driven by

values and necessity. Taking the Bible as a starting point (approximately 1450 BC), the precept

of the sanctity of human life explained earlier in the Noahic Covenant stands in sharp contrast to

---

[19]Sun Tzu, *The Art of War,* Translated by Samuel Griffith (London: Oxford University Press, 1971), 58.
[20]Sun Tzu, 59.
[21]Vincent Brooks, personal interview with the author, Ft. Leavenworth, Kansas, April 5, 2006.

Sun Tzu's writing in its value of human life. The earlier precept concerning murder is reinforced later in the Bible when God gives the Decalogue to Abraham. These Ten Commandments were to be explicitly adhered to by the Children of Israel as an expression of the absolute values of God. Even so, based upon the Biblical record, populations were treated with the most extreme measures. Populations, as in the aforementioned Canaanite nations, were utterly destroyed or enslaved, but the consequences of Biblical warfare were based upon Judeo ethic as set down in the laws of the Torah, which later for Christians became the Old Testament of the Bible. These laws represented the stated values of Israel and can be pointed to as the justification for the manner in which populations were treated. The consequences of war as experienced by conquered populations elsewhere in the ancient world was much the same.

In addition to the Bible, one can look to Thucydides and the Peloponnesian Wars (431-405 BC) to pick up the thread of government reasoning based upon accepted values that were used in justifying military action. Here in Book I, Chapters IV and V, one finds delegations of Corinthians, Corcyraeans, Athenians, and Spartans stating their case before each other as they jockey for allegiances through the justification of their past acts of military aggression. These various political argumentations were based upon an excepted system of values from which each party reasoned his cause to be just. In part, the system of values that guided the political rhetoric of the time can be seen in the writings of Aristotle and Plato. In Book V of the works of Aristotle concerning politics and the causes of revolution, he speaks of the accepted norm of justice and proportionate equality among governments. Aristotle goes on to state that in democracies these ideas are based upon "the notion that those who are equal in any respect are equal in all respects; because men are equally free they claim to be absolutely equal."[22] Regardless of the lofty

---

[22]Aristotle, *Book V*, 1.

political rhetoric, during the ancient era of warfare the people were at the mercy of warring armies and seen as a material part of the spoils of war rather than military objectives themselves.

Later in the ancient era, one sees people being treated much the same when Rome deals with the Jewish revolts and the destruction of Jerusalem in 70 AD. Josephus' works describe continuous revolts and insurrections in detail. His description of the destruction of Jerusalem and the Temple are noteworthy because the city was destroyed by Roman Legionnaires during the Jewish Passover celebration. Jerusalem, which had been conquered five times and destroyed once previously, had never been attacked during one of its most revered religious festivals. Because it was Passover, there were well over a million visitors who were trapped in the city when it was besieged by the Romans.[23] Again, the main point is that populations were treated with absolute, brutal measures. The remarks by Josephus about how the Roman soldiers simply tired of slaughtering the men of the city[24] brings a sharp contrast to today's universally accepted value of human life and liberty .

In contrast to how Rome dealt with Jerusalem, one may look to the writings of Saint Augustine a little more than three centuries later. Saint Augustine wrote the *City of God* in the early fifth century from a deep understanding of both the Greek philosophies and Biblical writings. Augustine expounds upon the positive influence Christianity had on the barbarians attacking Rome and the subsequent treatment of the citizens caught between the armies. Here in chapter seven, referring to events that took place during the Visigoths' sacking of Rome, Augustine relates that it was unprecedented for the basilicas to be set aside as places of safety for the city's refugees to gather. He also mentions that these refugees were to be given immunity and protection from execution, rape, or captivity and that many of them had been actually led there by

---

[23]Josephus, *The Complete Works* (Nashville: Thomas Nelson Publishers, 1998), 6.9.2-6.10.1.
[24]Josephus, 6.9.2.

the enemy.[25] The change in the behavior of armies at war, especially during the sacking of a wealthy city, shows that Christianity with its accompanying system of values influenced the ethics of war. A key point in relation to Augustine's *City of God* is that it was written a century after the Roman Emperor Constantine had decreed that all citizens must accept Christianity as the official religion. Constantine's decree was made official with the Edict of Milan in 313 AD and the Council of Nicea in 325 AD. While the value of human life seemed to be improving, the changes that took place were still fully within the jurisdiction of governments and militaries; they did not generate from the consensus of the people in mass or through pressure placed on the political decision maker by the people. St. Augustine wrote *The City of God,* in part, to refute the argument that the influence of Christianity and departure from the old Roman gods had caused Rome's downfall. The fact that St. Augustine has to refute this argument, and that Emperor Constantine adopted Christianity despite the people's desires to continue to worship the Roman gods, reveals that the citizenry's influence on political decision makers was limited.

When one turns one's attention to the people and considers unconventional warfare, it becomes clear that unconventional or irregular warfare has also been around since the beginning of human history, but not as the decisive form of warfare. Darius the Great, King of Persia and his son Xerxes I, The Great (558-465 BC collectively), Alexander the Great (356-323 BC), and the ancient Roman Empire (31 BC-476 AD) all dealt with insurgencies. The rebellion of the Greek states against Alexander, initiated through the use of information operations and deception, is a good early example of irregular warfare.

Demosthenes circulated and promoted a rumor that Alexander had been killed while fighting against the Illyrian tribes. Demosthenes, who actually produced an eyewitness to Alexander's death, was able to raise money for a revolt in Thebes. This resulted in Alexander's

---

[25]Saint Augustine, *City of God* (New York: Image Books by Doubleday, 1958), 44.

immediate offensive into Greece and capture of Thebes followed by its subsequent destruction and the enslavement of its surviving citizenry.[26] Two points about Alexander's experience with the Greek revolts are noteworthy. First, the fact that the single piece of information about Alexander's supposed death when placed in the information environment of the time, created a powerful enough perception to embolden insurrectionists to act. Demosthenes' actions beg the question: what would have happened throughout Alexander's empire had this disinformation been circulated overnight to his entire realm and to his many neighboring enemies? Secondly, Alexander's response of razing Thebes to the ground and selling the surviving citizenry into slavery was absolute in its effectiveness against the insurgents and absolutely unacceptable in today's world where one of the universally held tenants is human rights.

Two major factors that influenced the flow of information during these time periods were the rural agricultural lifestyle and the lack of change in the technology of communication. The transfer of information was restricted to human, horse or sail networks, and the resultant speed of communicating detailed information remained relatively the same from the Ancient through Gunpowder Era. Speed of communication was increased through engineering projects such as the Roman road networks and through increased and better-coordinated use of the horse, as in the case of Genghis Khan's Mongol army. But, while these helped maximize the ability to move information as quickly as humanly possible, the relative time it took for the transfer of information across continents (not to mention the known world) had its limit.

Rudimentary means of signaling, such as smoke signals, drums, watch fires, heliograph (mirrors), and semaphore (flags), have been used throughout history. These forms of information transfer were limited in their ability to send detailed information and were usually kept within the control of governments and armies and not widely used by people in general. The first formal

---

[26]John Warry, *Warfare in the Classical World* (New York: Barnes and Noble Books, 2000), 99.

courier system recorded in history was used by the Pharaohs of Egypt around 2400 BC and the

first formal postal system is attributed to Cyrus the Great, King of Persia in 550 BC.[27] To get a

sense of time related to the transfer of information over a formalized courier system, one can look

to Roman history. A.M. Ramsey determined that the speed of the Roman post overland from

Rome to Egypt, about 3,177 miles, in 193 AD was about sixty-three days or approximately sixty

miles per day.[28] Homing pigeons have been used since 1150 AD in the Middle East and are still

used today in remote areas of India as a means of communicating emergency information

following natural disasters. But again, even though it has become possible to send more than a

small note tied to the pigeon's leg, the amount of information and efficiency of using homing

pigeons is limited.[29] When one thinks of the speed and diffusion of information during this era,

and considers the fact that populations were primarily agriculturally based, the limited ability of

the affects of information on the mobilization of populations as a part of the political process

becomes evident.

The Medieval and Gunpowder Eras of War

The Medieval Era of warfare began with the fall of Rome in 476 AD and lasted to the

middle of the 1400's when gunpowder came into widespread use. The Gunpowder Era of

Warfare began in the mid 15th century up to the start of the Industrial Revolution between the 18th

and early 19th centuries. Transition from the Ancient to Medieval and Medieval to Gunpowder

Eras of Warfare were marked by three areas of change important to this study: first, technological

innovations that forced revolutions in military affairs; second, the affects of Reformation and

---

[27]Wikipedia, *Mail* [document online]; available from http://en.wikipedia.org/ , Internet, accessed on January 24, 2006.
[28]Wikipedia, *Cusus publicu* [document online]; available from http://en.wikipedia.org , Internet, accessed on January 24, 2006.
[29]Wikipedia, *Homing pigeon* [document online]; available from http://en.wikipedia.org , Internet, accessed on January 24, 2006.

Humanist thinking on the development of Western Civilization; and third, the rise of the nation state.

The single technological advance that had the power to affect large numbers of people simultaneously was the invention of the printing press, first in China and later during the 15th century by Johann Gutenberg of Germany. This invention marks the first major event affecting the evolution of mass media. By the end of the 15th century most cities throughout Europe, as well as in the Muslim territories in southern Gaul, had printing presses. Through printings of political, theological, philosophical, and economic writings, it was possible to begin to influence the thinking of groups of people and build popular consensus. Although the medium that could affect popular consensus now existed, production and distribution of printed materials was still not fast enough to affect the nature of war. At this time, in relation to the new mass media audience, a perception of the 'action to value connection' was still not a significant factor affecting how armies conducted warfare. Another critical area to be affected with the advent of the printing press was education. With an exponential infusion of the printed word, made available to anybody who had the money to purchase a book or tract, came the desire to know how to read. The seed was planted that would eventually produce widespread education for the lower and middle classes. With the spread of education came the sharing of power. The Church throughout the Middle Ages maintained control of print and was the primary means of education, but mainly for the upper classes and theologians of the day. The distribution of the printed word made it possible for people to seek education outside of the jurisdiction of the Church which meant that the Church lost one of her main sources of power – control over knowledge.

Major technological advances directly affecting how wars were conducted included: 1) the stirrup, revolutionizing the use of cavalry by enabling riders to use a growing assortment of weapons without being unseated; 2) siege craft; and 3) gunpowder, with which came the use of cannons and firearms that would eventually defeat both armor and stone fortifications.[30] Volumes have been written on historical revolutions in military affairs based upon the technological innovations of weaponry and equipment, but the main effects of these changes were on the evolution of how war was conducted on the battlefield and only enhanced the mil to mil dominance of the nature of war. When one looks to the theorists during these eras of war, one sees a refinement of the mil to mil art with almost no emphasis on the people as a integral part of the execution of warfare. Machiavelli's *The Art of War*, Fredrick the Great's instructions to his commanders, and Jomini's *The Art of War* all deal much more with military leadership and formations, the most effective use and combination of weapons, and logistical considerations than they did with the relationship and influence of people on the conduct of war.

In considering the values that framed the thinking of governments during these periods, an understanding of the Protestant Reformation of the 16th century is critical. Much like America's Founding Fathers would defy the authority of England's King some three hundred years later, the Reformers, such as Germany's Martin Luther, France's John Calvin, and Switzerland's Ulrich Zwingli[31], defied the authority of the Pope of the Roman Catholic Church. The argument was the same: God's authority supercedes human authority. For the Reformers this was articulated in the argument that the Bible was ultimately the only authority by which man's conscience could be bound: *Sole Scriptura* (Scripture Alone). Luther, arguing against Erasmus' Diatribe on the Freedom of the Will, quotes the Bible from Proverbs: "The king's heart is in the hand of the Lord...He turneth it withersoever He will,"[32] stating that "it is the most active

---

[30]Wikipedia, *Medieval warfare* [document online]; available from http://en.wikipedia.org , Internet, accessed on January 28, 2006.

[31]B. K. Kuiper, *The Church in History* (Grand Rapids, MI: WM. B. Eerdmans Publishing Co., 1993), 182-192.

[32]Proverbs 21:1, KJV.

operation of God, which man cannot avoid or alter."[33] John Calvin adds to this in his argument against Pighius stating that "the law, however, was given not to bear witness to man's power but rather to prove his weakness, so that, having been reminded by the commandment that he can do nothing, he may rest on God's strength, not his own."[34] It was the appeal to God's authority over and against the then corrupt Roman Catholic Church that shook the foundations of the institutional state authorities of the day. Dr. Francis Schaeffer's seminal work, *How Should We Then Live? The Rise and Decline of Western Thought and Culture,* thoroughly deals with the influences of Reformation versus Enlightenment thought on the West. He shows a strong contrast between the strength of the American Constitution, which, he argues was based upon an understanding of absolutes, understood through Judeo-Christian ethic, versus the post-French Revolution attempts to write an equally binding document based on predominantly humanistic philosophic thought.[35] Insight is gained of the teleological side of the Clausewitzian trinity: reason, passion, and chance, through an understanding of what framed the thinking and defined the values for people during these pivotal periods of history. The combination of mass media through the printed word and the ideas of freedom from oppressive or unjust authority derived from Reformation and Humanistic thought, to borrow Thomas Friedman's term, 'superempowered' the common man of the day and set conditions for revolution. What ensued were religious wars including the Hussite Wars in Bohemia (1420-34), the Thirty Years' War in what is now Germany (1618-1648), as well other wars, such as the American Revolutionary War (1775-83) and the French Revolution (1789-99). The Peace of Westphalia that marked the end of the Thirty Years' War also marked the emergence of the modern system of states, which still applies today.

---

[33]Martin Luther, *The Bondage of the Will,* translated by J.I. Packer and O.R. Johnston (Grand Rapids, MI: Revell of Baker Book House Co., 2003), 258-259.

[34]John Calvin, *The Bondage and Liberation of the Will,* Ed. By A.N.S. Lane, Translated by G.I. Davies (Grand Rapids, MI: Baker Books, 2002), 208.

Although the emphasis in the conduct of warfare remained mil to mil, the nexus of nationalistic identity together with the superempowerment of the individual that came with Reformation and Humanistic thought, brought to life the 'passion' component of the Trinity. The convergence of these dynamics together with the use of the new advances in military technology culminated with the French Revolution and the Napoleonic Wars between 1792 and 1815. The compounding affects of unique circumstances, which included the wide acceptance of the humanistic ideas of the Enlightenment along with economic depression and the rise of the bourgeoisie, led to revolution in France and the end of its *ancien régime*. The institution of the *levee en masse* combined with Napoleon's technique of military promotion, based upon service and performance rather than political or social position, enabled the French to field a new kind of army: an army that was supposed to be for the people, and by the people; an army that seemed unstoppable to the smaller more traditional European militaries.

The French monarchy lost the allegiance of the people because it did not act consistent with social values. This perceived disconnect eventually led to the French Revolution and massive social disorder as France transitioned to democracy and republicanism. But, the need for a strong military dominated France's reconstructive process. The awareness of, and ability to combine these dynamic social, technological, and military changes of the time marked Napoleon Bonaparte as a leader without peer and one of the great Captains in military history. While Napoleon seemed to be the first to identify and harness these powerful dynamics, the fact that they were shaping the way in which nations would vie for domination or maintain political status-quo was taking shape throughout Western Civilization.

While a sense of nationalism among populations grew, along with a new infused sense of individual empowerment, it would be the technological advances in the area of communications

---

[35]Schaeffer, 124-128.

during the Industrial Era that would begin to affect warfare in a way that previously was not possible. Although the argument can be made in the cases of the Peninsular War that Napoleon ultimately lost, and the American Revolution that England ultimately forfeited, that the revolutionary power of disenfranchised populations are strong enough to be decisive against regular militaries in the field, it must be pointed out in both cases that the balance of power was tipped in favor of the populations by outside military support: the British Navy in the case of the Peninsular War and a combination of the French Navy and Army in the case of the American Revolution. Still, these cases, along with the Hussite War, Thirty Years' War, and other conflicts, such as the Bloodless Revolution that overthrew James II of England in 1688, are critical to the argument in this study because they represent a precursor on a smaller scale of the affect that can be achieved through the diffusion of new thoughts and ideas through the information environment; affects that were to be multiplied in the Industrial Era and are currently being exponentially exploded in the Information Age.

CHAPTER 2: The Industrial Era of War

The Industrial Era of warfare began with the Industrial Revolution in the late 18th century and lasted until the early 1980s. This time period within military history saw the convergence of nationalism, industrialization and urbanization, along with the massive conscription of armies and the dynamic influences of steam transportation, the rail, the telegraph, and wireless communication. An overwhelming flood of emergent medical, scientific, and industrial technologies marked this era as a time of great expectations for humanity. Figure 3 shows the relative changes that occurred during the industrial age depicted within the Clausewitzian trinity (hereafter in this study the Clausewitzian Trinity is referred to as the 'CT').

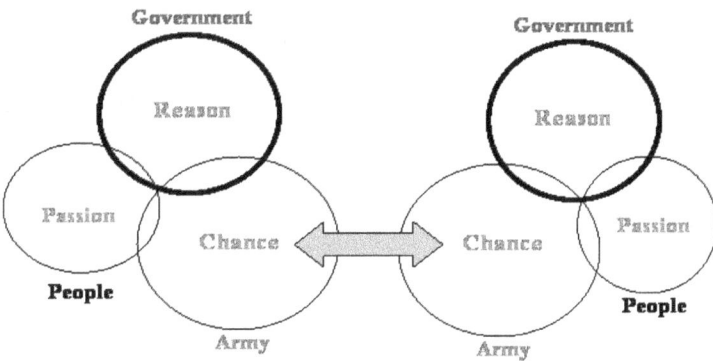

Figure 3. The Influence of Information Flow Begins to Change How Wars Are Fought

Again, the sizes of the circles represent the dominance or importance of each of the components in regards to decisiveness in the conduct and outcome of warfare. As in Figure 2, the people are the least important, but their importance is growing stronger as they are empowered by nationalistic identity, education and the increased flow of information. The government is still second in order of relevance, but the necessity to exercise reason based upon the accepted system of nation states with its accompanying values has become a much more significant factor in the conduct of warfare. Finally, the army, as in the previous three eras, is still the overall decisive

24

component in the nature of war. With the Industrial Age, however, came the emergence of revolutionary warfare as well as 'small wars' as competitors to conventional warfare. Three main points are emphasized in the analysis of the Industrial Era of War: the decisive component of warfare was still the military, the changes in how populations were dealt with, and how information flow began to dynamically affect the overall conduct of war. Of key importance will be an analysis of the area of perceptions created through the use of the information environment.

The Crimean War (1854-56) is an excellent example of how technological advances in weaponry and information flow, combined with the power of nationalism, affected the conduct of warfare. Fought on the Crimean Peninsula between Imperial Russia and the allied forces of the French, English, and Turks, this war marked one of the first examples of the use of the steamship for troop transportation, the rifled musket, and the telegraph. The ease with which the British and French were able to move troops into the theater of operations by steamship foreshadowed a mobility that had never before been enjoyed or imagined. The new rifled musket, perhaps the single most devastating technological advance at the time, was used by the English and French forces and caused a casualty ratio of four to one against the Russian forces who continued to mass in columns for the attack as per the dictates of the previous eras of warfare. While both of these examples affected the ability to shape and operate within the physical battlefield, the use of the telegraph began to directly influence the strategic direction of the war based upon how actions and conditions were reported and perceived back home.

For the first time in history, a foreign theater of operations was linked by telegraph to its homeland government. Heads of state were able to communicate back and forth with their field commanders with unprecedented speed, and newspaper reporters were able to get front line stories to the paper in days versus weeks.[36] There were two interesting outcomes of the new

information connectivity that technology brought to the Crimean War. First, the reason for going

to war against Imperial Russia was not strong enough to mobilize the new nationalistic power of

the European nation states. Regardless of the almost over-night reporting of the sufferings and

drama of the battlefield, the need to wage war was not perceived by the people of France and

England to be important enough to field armies for total war.[37] This is a crucial point because it

brings to the surface the government's responsibility to the people of its country when a decision

to expend blood and treasure must be made. The Crimean War was seen as a conflict over

obscure issues that were not critical to the survival of those nations.[38] Because the war was not

seen as necessary to national survival (not meeting one of the criteria for 'just war') there was an

absence of growing national fervor and mobilization in support of the war. Secondly, the

newspaper reporting, while not compelling enough to sustain or create nationalistic support for

the war, did force the government to initiate much-needed improvements for the common soldier

within the British army, as noted by Williamson Murray,

> [T]he time when senior officers could ignore the plight of common soldiers had passed.
> British correspondents reported the dreadful conditions under which the army was
> suffering, and the public outcry resulted in substantial reforms that began the process of
> modernizing the British army.[39]

While the Crimean War revealed the new dynamic within the relationship of the CT, with

political leaders communicating with their generals on the one hand, while on the other justifying

their actions to a better informed public, the American Civil War (1861-65) five years later would

fully expose just how powerful this new ability to communicate could be. As one analyzes the

Civil War with the CT in mind, each of the components comes vividly alive. The purpose of the

---

[36]Geoffrey Parker, Ed., *Cambridge Illustrated History, Warfare* (Cambridge, UK: Cambridge University Press, 2004), 218.
   [37]Parker, 218.
   [38]Parker, 219

war was based upon the issue of the state's right to self-govern and slavery, showing that the understanding of liberty and the sanctity and equality of human life had become important enough to go to war over. The slave population was the strategic center of gravity that the Confederacy fought to protect. The economic system of the Confederate States was dependent upon the slave population for labor. Using slave labor, however, did not square with the values set forth in the *Declaration of Independence;* there existed a painful disconnect between actions and stated values that was evident to many among the political leadership of the Northern States. While the practice of slavery was introduced into the colonies by Britain, some thirty years before the Civil War, through the efforts of William Wilberforce and others in Parliament, England passed the Slavery Abolition Act outlawing slavery in all of her territories. John Quincy Adams, perhaps the most ardent anti-slavery American President and Congressman, labored tirelessly in the years after his Presidency to have slavery abolished in all of the State. The former President indefatigably argued that "the inconsistency of the institution of domestic slavery with the principles of the Declaration of Independence was seen and lamented by all the southern patriots of the Revolution."[40]

The Emancipation Proclamation can be seen as an attempted direct attack on the strategic center of gravity of the Confederacy through the information environment. President Lincoln passed the proclamation on the heels of the battle of Antietam, considered the bloodiest single day of the Civil War, yet hailed as a Union victory. The proclamation stated that "as of 1 January 1863 the slaves would be free in all territories that remained in rebellion."[41] President Lincoln had in affect done the same thing that Demosthenes attempted to do to Alexander the Great in the third century BC; he attacked the Confederacy indirectly through the targeting of a key

---

[39]Parker, 220.
[40]Stephen McDowell, *The Bible, Slavery, and America's Founders* [document online]; available from http://www.wallbuilders.com/index.htm, Internet, accessed 30 January 2006.
[41]Parker, 224.

population by using the information environment. This attack constituted a direct blow against the enemy's center of gravity by creating a perception in the minds of the people that made up the labor force of the South. When one considers the demographics of the South at the time of the Civil War, a population of 9 million people of whom 3 million were slaves, the power of this single information event becomes substantial. While the affects of this information event are arguable, the fact that it was used as a political means of influencing an ongoing war at the strategic level is significant.

In analyzing the government to military relationship, the importance of the development and influence of the telegraph is powerfully portrayed in President Lincoln's correspondences and relationships with his generals. As Commander-in-Chief, President Lincoln's influence on his commanding generals was more significant than any other American President during a time of war before or since. In the course of the war, through direct intervention sustained by daily telegraphs, Lincoln replaced generals McClellan, Pope, Burnside, Hooker, and Meade, finally settling on Ulysses S. Grant as overall commander of the Union Army. When contrasted to the exchange between Sun Tzu and King Ho-lü two thousand years earlier, one sees a profound change in the relationship between government and military. The strain that President Lincoln dealt with was generated by a sense of obligation to the people component of the CT. Whereas in antiquity the rights of the people were more often than not of no consequence, in 19th century warfare they had become paramount.

When one looks at the military component of the CT, the Civil War stands as America's bloodiest war ever fought. As in the Crimean War, outdated maneuver doctrine, which required opposing armies to mass formations and advance in the open, combined with advanced weapons technology, such as rifled muskets and later repeater rifles, created a battlefield casualty count that would leave more Americans dead than in any other US conflict in history. The casualty results in the Civil War foreshadowed what was to come a half century later in World War I.

Beyond the American Civil War, the World Wars stand as the most powerful historical military examples of the height of Industrial Era total war. The technological advances in weaponry profoundly changed the face of battle in World War I, and the subsequent advances in the interwar period caused a doctrinal explosion with the Blitz Krieg at the advent of WW II. The German offensive through the Ardennes forest into France hailed the advent of a new kind of warfare that combined the air and ground components of a nation's military in a fast-moving armor-based maneuver warfare. In an unprecedented six weeks, the German Army overwhelmed the Allies, almost destroyed the British Expeditionary Force on the beaches of Dunkirk, and forced the capitulation of France. Much like Napoleon's ability to harness the dynamics of nationalism and the technological advances of the Gunpowder Era, German military commanders were able to take the lessons learned from WW I and the technological advances of the industrial era and bring them together in May of 1940 against the supposedly impregnable Maginot Line. Although the Germans were not alone in understanding the implication of armor and the resurgence of maneuver warfare (for example Britain's B.H. Liddell Hart and J.F.C. Fuller had written extensively on it), they were the first to put theory into action with stunning results.

During the Industrial Era US experiences in Small Wars from 1840 to 1940, although still dominated by the military component of the CT, served to highlight the growing dynamics of unconventional war and how the media and perception began to play a more powerful role in warfare. The influence of the emerging press and information sharing can be seen in how the United States Marine Corps (USMC) experiences in the Second Caco War (1915-20) were reported in the information environment of the time. This time the issue wasn't one concerned with the suffering of the troops in extreme conditions as in the Crimean War, but of indigenous Haitians suffering at the hands of US forces. During this infamous war, among the many small wars that have been conducted in Haiti, a local Marine commander was pronounced insane and sent to an asylum for having two natives "shot to death just for the excitement of it."[42] Once this

event was placed in the information environment through a leak to the media about supposedly

widespread "indiscriminate killing,"[43] growing concern in the United States at the perception of

how the Marines were handling the situation in Haiti turned this event into an election issue for

presidential hopeful Warren G. Harding. Enough commotion was made by Harding that the issue

was picked up by the National Association for the Advancement of Colored People and other

powerful American lobbyists, leading to an eleven-month congressional investigation in 1922.[44]

Although the Marines were found innocent of indiscriminate killing, this example of tactical-level

ethics having strategic-level affect can easily be seen. While atrocities were committed by only a

few individual Marines in Haiti, the perception created in the minds of the American people by

the media, lobbyists and politicians was a distortion of the magnitude of what actually occurred.

While a recounting of this incident underscores the importance of ethically acceptable

behavior during the conduct of counterinsurgency, one cannot say that morally unethical behavior

has historically been a causative factor in the failure of counterinsurgencies. A recounting of just

a few such wars of the 19th and 20th centuries indicate that when conducted, counterinsurgencies

were more times than not successful. Counterinsurgencies carried out by Britain in the Second

Boer War, also known as The South African War, and by the American army in the Philippines,

interestingly in the same four year period from 1899 to 1902, were successful despite being noted

for atrocities committed by both the UK and US armies. History shows that although there has

always been a negative public reaction to armies committing unethical acts on the battlefield, it

does not show that in the past these reactions have been overly influential. However, in the

Information Era of the 21st century, the unwillingness of the people to support the unethical

conduct of counterinsurgent warfare, coupled with the ability to create global perceptions through

---

[42]Max Boot, *The Savage Wars of Peace* (New York: Basic Books, 2002), 176.
[43]Boot, 176.

unprecedented communications connectivity, has led to the emergence of the CT component of

'people' as much more decisive than in times past.

---

[44]Boot, 176-177.

CHAPTER 3: A Theory on the Dynamics of War in the 21st Century

> We have entered an age of constant conflict. Information is at once our core commodity and the most destabilizing factor of our time.[45]

In the previous chapter a correlation between technological advances and the decisive component of warfare has been shown. From the Ancient to the Gunpowder Era of warfare, which culminated with the invention of the printing press and the establishment of the nation state, the military component has been decisive. Following the Treaty of Westphalia and ascendancy of the nation state through the Industrial Era of Warfare, the military has maintained its overall dominance but has been controlled much more directly by government. With the end of the Cold War and the advent of the Information Era, the people component of the CT is becoming decisive and will increasingly begin to influence how wars will be fought. The dynamic that is driving warfare today, again borrowing from Friedman, "the thing that gives it its unique character,"[46] is *the speed and diffusion of information* down to the individual person on a global scale. The information itself in its electronic, written, visual, or audio form is the physical agent used to create perception in the minds of the people receiving it. Without information in the form of pictures, sounds and symbols, there is no affect or perception created that can actualize the people. The preceding chapter's historical overview of the flow and diffusion of information has shown its correlative effect on the conduct of warfare. It is the 'quickening' of this same relationship that is beginning to drive the way war is being fought today and will be fought in the future. Figure 4 shows an overview of the key technological developments pertaining to information throughout history and their effects on the relationship of the

---

[45]Ralph Peters, *Fighting for the Future, Will America Triumph?* (Mechanicsburg, PA: Stackpole Books, 2001), 133.

[46]Thomas Friedman, *The World is Flat* (New York, NY: Farrar, Straus and Giroux, 2005), 9.

components of the CT. A correlation can be drawn between technological advances in communication and the controlling or decisive component of the CT.

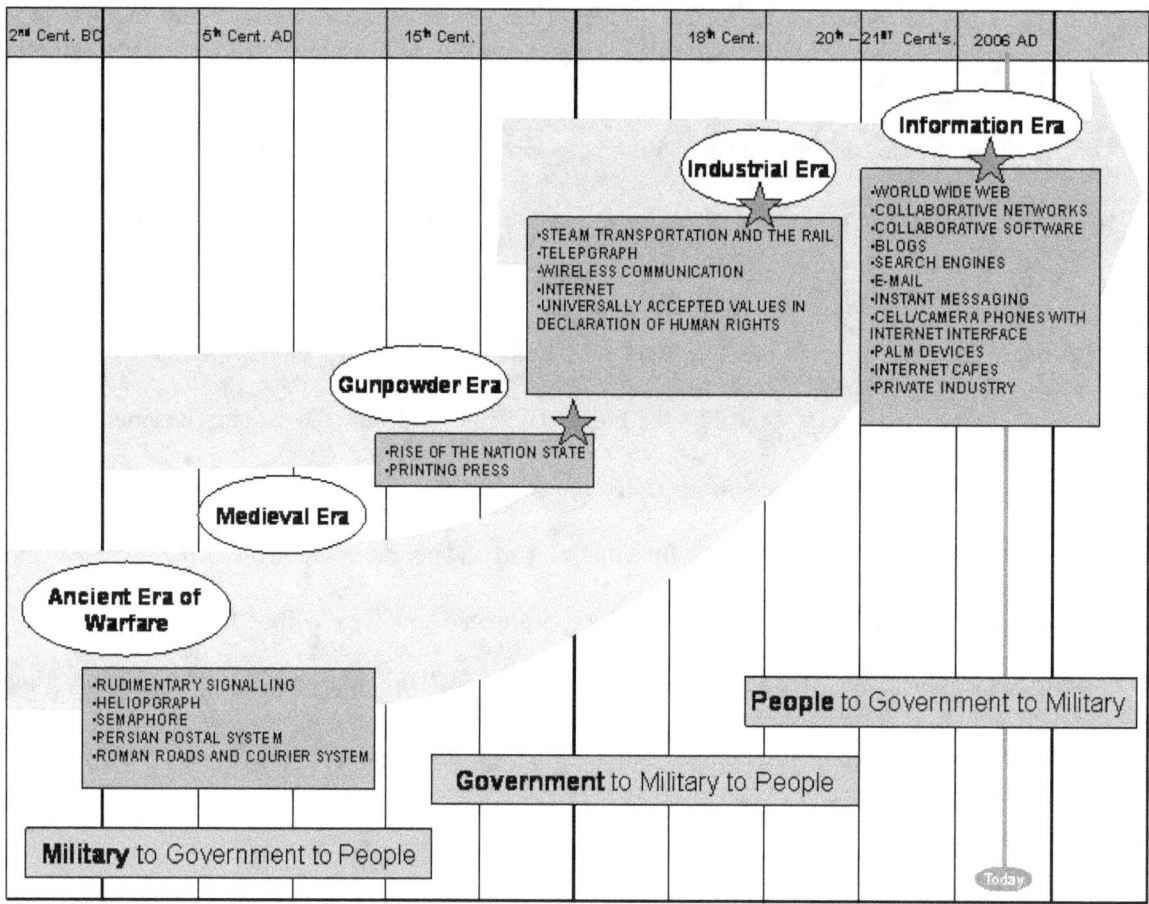

Figure 4. The Effects of Information on the Nature of Warfare throughout History

In the Ancient Era militaries dominated because the means by which people were influenced through information was limited. In the Gunpowder Era with the rise of the nation state and the invention of the printing press, government became more decisive in its role as mediator between the people, their army, and other nations. The printing press brought with it the capability of informing the public through mass media and greatly enhanced their new-found nationalistic identity. The dynamics that began in the Gunpowder Era were strengthened through the Industrial Era as powerful new means of communications were invented. In the Information

Era, the technological advances that make up the information environment have actualized the people component of the CT in a way never before experienced in history. As events unfold on the battlefield and are instantaneously reported in the information environment, perceptions are created that can affect the outcome of the war. Because of the power of perception, *Information Operations* (IO) has become an overarching line of operation in the conduct of war.

Three forces have converged in the information environment to greatly increase the importance of the 'people' component of the CT. These are: 1) the technological advances that have greatly increased, and are continuing to increase exponentially, the speed and diffusion of information; 2) the opening-up of free-market enterprise to the entire world as argued by Thomas Friedman in *The World Is Flat*, and Martin Van Creveld in *The Rise and Decline of the State*; and 3) the global consensus of acceptable conduct based upon the values outlined in the Universal Declaration of Human Rights and other internationally accepted bodies of law. These three forces synergistically make up the powerful phenomenon that is actualizing the people component of warfare. The new decisiveness of the 'people' component of the CT represents the central difference in how wars will be fought in the future; a warfare that must grapple with the powerful dynamic of a socially networked world.

Technological Advances

In 1997 Dorothy and Peter Denning noted that within a ten-year period the internet had grown from one-third of one percent of its initial size to a world wide web of over fifty million users with access virtually anywhere on earth.[47] They argued that the internet had become a globally interconnected network that represents not a technical phenomenon but a social one.[48] The importance of the understanding that this is a social phenomenon is foundational to

---

[47] Dorothy Denning and Peter Denning, *Internet Besieged, Countering Cyberspace Scofflaws* (Boston: Addison-Wesley Professional, 1997), 1.

understanding what the future holds for warfare. In a presentation at Ft. Leavenworth, a high

ranking military official from the National Security Agency related the following statistics: by the

end of 2006, 62 billion e-mails are expected to be sent daily, and by the end of 2007, over 1,380

billion instant messages; there are currently over 1.5 billion mobile phone users and over 2 billion

are projected by 2007; and internet users will increase from 1 billion in 2005 to over 1.3 billion in

2007. The US Department of Commerce reported that internet traffic doubles every 100 days and

"the rate of adoption of the Internet is eclipsing that of all other technologies preceding it. It took

38 years for radio and 13 years for television to achieve this level of acceptance."[49]

Software components that are enhancing the diffusion and sharing of information are

formal and informal collaborative networks such as the US Army's CompanyCommand.Net, a

collaborative forum for professionals to network and share lessons learned on a single internet

sight regardless of the member's location. Collaborative forums, together with micro-technology

hardware that is increasingly affordable, such as personal computers, cell phones with camera and

internet interface, and palm devices, have exploded access to the commercial communications

marketplace. The global collaborative power this technology has provided is unprecedented with

far-reaching implications that can only be guessed. It is not uncommon today for gamers (video

game players) to be networked together from America to Japan to Denmark sharing in ongoing

games made possible by sophisticated interactive software. These software capabilities include

real-time audio and visual that allows participants to actually see and talk to each other through

live feeds while they are gaming. These are just a few examples of the connectivity and

collaboration possible today via the information environment. When one considers networking

---

[48]Dorothy and Peter Denning, 11-12.

[49]Kim Sheehan and Mariea Hoy, *Using E-mail To Survey Internet Users In The United States: Methodology And Assessment,* Journal of Computer-Mediated Communication, Vol. 4, Issue 3, March 1999 [document online]; available from http://jcme.indiana.edu/vol4/issue3/sheehan.html, Internet accessed 5 February 2006.

through the use of the information environment, the concept of creating regional and global

perceptions that may affect the battle-space is conceivable.

A Globalized Free-Market Enterprise

When one looks to the business world and the free-market system, the power of

globalization becomes vividly apparent. Thomas Friedman's book, *The World is Flat*, should

make military planners sit up and take notice. This book offers a look into the corporate world of

global business in regard to technological advances and free-market enterprise. What is revealed

in Friedman's research is beyond revolutionary in comparison to what has been written

concerning Revolutions in Military Affairs (RMA's) of the past. Friedman writes that,

> [T]he dynamic force in globalization 3.0 – the thing that gives it its unique character – is
> the newfound power for *individuals* to collaborate and compete globally. And the lever
> that is enabling individuals and groups to go global so easily and so seamlessly is not
> horsepower, not hardware, but software – all sorts of new applications – in conjunction
> with the creation of a global fiber-optic network that has made us all next-door
> neighbors.[50]

Again, the technological advances of software applications and global fiber-optic

connectivity referred to by Friedman have to do with connectivity and the sharing of information.

What he has learned through extensive travel and research is that opportunities to exploit the

marketplace are becoming possible for more and more people: not just countries and

corporations, but people, because of informational connectivity on a global scale. He has shown

that through the outsourcing of specialized niche capabilities, much of the ancillary services

required in today's industry are being dominated by private businesses located in countries that in

the past were considered Third World. When one considers how this may affect the conduct of

warfare, Pakistan comes to mind. Economically, Pakistan has joined the tide of outsourcing

software technologies, grabbing a piece of the market from her neighbor India, which strongly caters to the U.S. software-technology industry. The Karachi based information technologies firm, System Innovations, made $10 million in sales in 2005, and is looking forward to tripling in size in the next 12 months.[51] The company will do this by boosting sales to North American corporations, which will include opening offices in Texas and Ontario. Another company, Lahore's Techlogix, one of Pakistan's first software exporters, gets 95 percent of its business from the U.S., most of which is relayed to 90 software developers in Pakistan from a four-member team stationed in Boston.[52] As developing corporate networks grow and strengthen in both Pakistan and India, it will become increasingly important for US Military planners to understand how these systems may affect the battlefield. In the current war on terror, Al Qaeda insurgent networks crisscross the entire region, including Afghanistan, Pakistan and India. Understanding corporate networks and their nodal relationship to the local tribal and religious demographics of these countries has already become critical.

Universally Acknowledged Values

The effects of globalization have led to an increased awareness and consensus of universally acknowledged values that have been championed by the UN, and are now being enforced through NATO's ability to project military power. Since the establishment of the League of Nations in 1919 and its replacement, the United Nations (UN) after WW II, the influence of international bodies of governance has increased. The UN, as an association of governments, facilitates cooperation in international law, security, economic development, and social equity. Currently the UN consists of 191 member states "including virtually all

---

[50]Friedman, 9.
[51]Naween Mangi, *Pakistan: Better Late Than Never in Outsourcing*, Business Week online, 9 May 2005 [document online]; available from http://www.businessweek.com/ , Internet, accessed 11 February 2006.
[52]Naween Mangi.

internationally recognized independent nations."[53] Justification for taking military action within the world community today almost always depends on consensus gained through the UN. Besides the threat of an Iraqi weapon of mass destruction program, much of President Bush's justification for going to war in Iraq in 2003 was based upon Iraq's consistent violations of UN resolutions over the last decade since the first Gulf War. Furthermore, it was through UN weapons inspection teams that continued efforts to ascertain Saddam Hussein's compliance to the resolutions was sought. UN peacekeeping forces comprised of various multinational coalitions of forces have deployed to literally hundreds of locations around the world to monitor and enforce peace, as well as to provide security and humanitarian aid throughout the Third World.

As noted in the introduction of this study, the Universal Declaration of Human Rights (UDHR) embodies principles that have been agreed upon by most signatory members of the United Nations and is one of the most widely used tools for applying diplomatic and moral pressure on governments. Although it is not a legally binding document, it does serve as the foundation for the "original two legally-binding UN human rights Covenants, the *International Covenant on Civil and Political Rights,* and the *International Covenant on Economic, Social, and Cultural Rights,*" and is widely referred to by academics and constitutional courts.[54] While in the past the UN has often been criticized as an inept, powerless body, it does represent an international forum for debate on the conduct of warfare. Furthermore, since the end of the Cold War the UN has gained influence and increased authority through organizations that have the power to enforce their charters. Two such organizations are NATO (North Atlantic Treaty Organization) and the European Union's (EU) new rapid reaction force.

---

[53]Wikipedia, *United Nations* [document online]; available from http://en.wikipedia.org/ , Internet, accessed on February 15, 2006.
[54]Wikipedia, *Universal Declaration of Human Rights* [document online]; available from http://en.wikipedia.org/wiki/Declaration_of_human_rights , Internet, accessed on February 15, 2006.

The human rights atrocities committed in Kosovo through Slobodan Milosevic's policies of ethnic cleansing demonstrate an evolution in the purpose of existing international bodies, such as NATO, when they are operating under the auspices of UN charters and mandates. Paddy Ashdown, a soldier serving with the UN, recounts time he spent in an Albanian refugee camp on the Kosovo border where a young woman said to him, "I was always told the west only went to war for land or oil, yet here is NATO fighting for me."[55] Ashdown goes on to discuss a contradiction in purposes by quoting the UN's position of non-interference in issues concerning the internal domestic affairs of a recognized sovereign as stated in Article 2, Paragraph 7 of the UN Charter, and he concludes with an unsettled question pertaining to the evolving post-Cold War role of NATO. In noting that "Kosovo was arguably the first war in which the refugees became the purpose of the war,"[56] the traditional territorial issues of sovereignty seem to have taken a back-seat to fighting for the principle of human rights.

More recently NATO has taken on a new role in the War on Terror with its current responsibility for providing Provincial Reconstruction Teams (PRTs) in Afghanistan. "NATO is currently in the process of filling the requirements for expansion of ISAF (International Security Assistance Force) to the West (within Afghanistan), with a view to establish new PRTs, as well as to incorporate existing PRTs, currently under the command of the US-led Coalition." (parenthetical note added by author)[57] The implications of this new role for NATO are far reaching. NATO represents an international organization established for mutual defense collaboration that is evolving from its Cold-War charter of self defense. Its new charter includes the task of functioning as a capable expeditionary force that can intervene anywhere in the world in extreme cases of human rights violations.

---

[55]Patrick Mileham and L. Willet, Eds., *Military Ethics for the Expeditionary Era* (London: The Royal Institute of International Affairs, 2002), 11.
[56]Mileham and Willets, 11.

Perhaps the most significant example of the necessity for internationally accepted statements of value is the Cairo Declaration of Human Rights in Islam (CDHRI). The drafting and ratification of this significant declaration, by the 19th Conference of Foreign Ministers in Cairo on 5 August 1990, established Shariah law as the only source of reference for the protection of human rights in Islamic countries. In the view of the 57 member states of the Organization of the Islamic Conference (OIC),[58] the acknowledgement of this declaration established its supremacy over the UDHR [Universal Declaration of Human Rights, articles 24 and 25], based on the divine revelation of the writings of Mohammed and the Qur'an.[59] The necessity of such a document became increasingly apparent to UN representatives of Islamic states, such as the Rajaie-Khorassani of Iran, who stated that the UDHR "could not be implemented by Muslims and did not accord with the system of values recognized by the Islamic Republic of Iran."[60] As in the Biblical justification for the destruction of the enemies of Israel, the Reformers' dispute against the Catholic Church of the 14th and 15th centuries, and the Founding Fathers' reasoning for carrying out the American Revolution in the 18th century, the OIC today is appealing to what they believe is a higher authority. The OIC holds up the CDHRI, which is based upon the writings of Mohammed and the Qur'an, over what they perceive to be a wholly secular document.

There are apparent differences between the 1948 version of the UDHR and the newly drafted CDHRI, in regards to defining what universally accepted human rights should be. Despite these differences, in 1997 the CDHRI received a UN stamp of approval, according to David G. Littman of the UN Commission on Human Rights, "when published in volume II... *A*

---

[57]Global Security.org, *Provincial Reconstruction Teams (PRTs)* [document online]; available from http://www.globalsecurity.org/military/ops/oef-prt.htm, Internet accessed 17 February, 2006.

[58]Infoplease, *The Organization of Islamic Conference Member States* [document online]; available from http://www.infoplease.com/spot/oicstates1.html, Internet, accessed 27 February 2006.

[59]David Littman, *Human Rights and Creeping Islamism at the United Nations,* lecture notes for the Advanced Operational Arts Studies Fellowship, The School of Advanced Military Studies, 6 October 2005, 5.

[60]Littman, 4.

Compilation of International Instruments, under the auspices of the Office of the UN High Commissioner for Human Rights."[61] The OIC's belief in the necessity of the CDHRI underscores the importance for states or groups of states to be able legitimize their actions based upon stated values. Furthermore, it validates the increasing importance of the sanctioning power of international bodies like the UN.

The Information Era of Warfare

People, through technological advances have been given the tools necessary to network globally. People, through the opening up of free-market enterprises made possible by software technologies and fiber-optic connectivity, have a stake in a globalized world economy. And, people, because of the increased influence of bodies such as the UN and networked collaborative forums on the World Wide Web, have an environment in which to be heard and to build consensus when a belligerent has attacked their state's sovereignty. When applied to warfare, especially counterinsurgent warfare, people, in general, have gained a much more prominent role in the conduct of war than in times past. If the people become disenfranchised from the counterinsurgent, then the war cannot be sustained regardless of the operational or tactical success of the army. Although the popular will of the people has always been an object of war, in the 21st century the methods of attaining the object have changed significantly.[62] Figure 5 depicts the people as the decisive component of the CT because they exist in a globalized world of connectivity that bypasses the traditional and more isolated relationship between a nation's people-government- and army.

---

[61]Littman, 6.

[62]Vincent Brooks, personal interview with the author, Ft. Leavenworth, Kansas, January 12, 2006. BG Vincent Brooks is the current Chief of the Army's Office of Public Affairs.

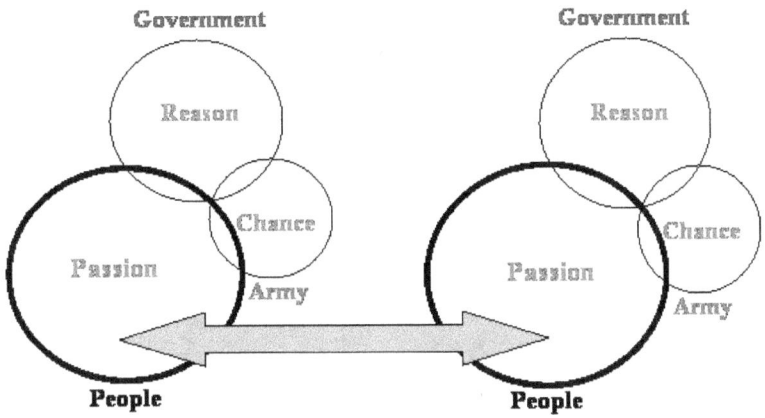

Figure 5. The Information Era of War

Today people have access to an interactive global network through which values, beliefs, and political perspective can be acquired and shared. The information environment will inform peoples' geopolitical understanding of the world to include both sides of the argument concerning the justness of waging war. A good example of this kind of geopolitical consensus was seen after President G.W. Bush and the US Congress made the decision to invade Iraq. The intense ridicule and backlash from traditional European allies, the same allies that had supported going into Afghanistan, was significant and powerful in its influence on how the world perceived the legitimacy of the decision to invade Iraq. Legitimacy, defined as the moral authority to act, is undermined significantly at all levels of war by heads of state, as well as soldiers and leaders that display unethical conduct. When a government makes a decision to go to war, be it conventional or unconventional, the war must be conducted in a manner that is consistent with that government's stated values. In the mass-media marketplace of the global information environment, the perception created by a country's decision to go to war (at the strategic level) or an isolated unethical action by a soldier on the ground (at the tactical level) can very quickly create perceptions on a global scale. The speed and diffusion of information, on a global scale, has moved the historic emphasis of warfare from how armies confront one another to how the

42

people of the world *perceive* such a confrontation. The perception of incidents of unethical behavior at all levels of war can and does have strategic-level impact.

Fortunately the dynamic speed and diffusion of information is a two-edged sword. Al-Qaeda and its affiliates have made their own blunders in the area of actions not lining up with values. The most recent example of an Al Qaeda blunder was the November 2005 bombing of hotels in Jordan which killed fifty-seven people and injured an additional three hundred. There was an immediate, intense negative reaction to these events throughout the Muslim world, most notably from Syria who has both passively and actively supported Al Qaeda. The confession of an Iraqi woman detained in connection with the bombings reinforced a negative perception of Al Qaeda that had been created among many in the Muslim world and seriously brought into question their radical fundamentalist position and what appeared to be a new direction for their attacks.

While the psychological effect of these information events serves to weaken the resolve of the perpetrators, it tends to strengthen that of the people or society on the receiving end of the action. Perceptions created through extreme examples of unethical behavior are difficult to correct and will not lose their potency for a very long time. When placed into the information environment, unethical actions at the tactical-level present a 'lose-lose' scenario for the perpetrator. The powerful images and written information of these incidents, which is diffused globally through the various communication conduits, erodes a perception of moral justness and legitimacy, hardens the resolve of the opponent, and weakens opportunities to gain support.[63]

Today, because information itself is the dynamic that influences the evolution of warfare, the non-physical aspects of warfare are being actualized. That is, the passion, reason, and chance of warfare are beginning to take on more emphasis than the physical ability to conduct warfare.

The physical aspect of war, which is currently dominated by the United States, is being challenged by the non-physical aspect of war fought in the information environment. The battle for popular will is becoming more decisive than a state's ability to dominate in a military to military engagement. Militaries are becoming smaller, more expeditionary, and more professional in order to conduct short-duration precision operations, while governments are spending more time and energy managing perceptions that are affecting a global society. The actions of militaries are being scrutinized by the global community in such a way that *how* they accomplish their missions has become just as important as successfully accomplishing their missions. More importantly, the playing field within the information environment is much more evenly matched than foes on the physical battlefield. The speed and diffusion of information and its effect on global or regional perception has become a crucial line of operation for governments and their militaries in the ethical conduct of warfare because there has occurred an "equalization of power" between state and non-state opponents.

In 1999, Martin Van Creveld argued that from 1500-1945 technology was essential in the construction of the state, but is now working against it. He said that modern technology causes power to be taken away from the state in favor of organizations that are neither territorially based nor in sovereignty altogether.[64] The speed with which the private-sector industry is evolving and globalizing should really cause the military planner to sit up and take notice. For military strategists, understanding the transition from the intensely competitive nature of the market place to that of the battlefield should not be difficult. As Friedman has noted:

> The playing field is not being leveled only in ways that draw in and superempower a whole new group of innovators. It's being leveled in a way that draw [*sic*] in and

---

[63]Caleb Carr, *Lessons of Terror, A History of Warfare Against Civilians: Why It Has Always Failed and Why It Will Fail Again* (New York: Random House, 2002), 223.

[64]Martin Van Creveld, *The Rise and Decline of the State* (Cambridge, UK: Cambridge University Press, 2002), 337.

superempowers a whole new group of angry, frustrated, and humiliated men and women.[65]

A great example of the combined influence of the media and the internet was seen after the 19 January 2006 release of an audiotape by Osama bin Laden. This example is significant because Osama bin Laden is a non-state actor heading the global Al Qaeda terrorist network, which has affiliates in each of the world's continents and is engaged in open warfare against the United States. In the audiotape Osama bin Laden recommends that people read the book *Rogue State* by William Blum to better understand President Bush's supposed lies and oppression. Dru Sefton, writing for *The Seattle Times*, reported that the evening after the audiotape release this book went from 209,000 to 27 on Amazon.com's sales list. She also reported that William Blum was an ex-State Department employee who has been speaking out against US foreign policy for 40 years.[66] Needless to say, Mr. Blum speaks out vehemently against the United States, claiming that "bombing, invasions, torture and weapons of mass destruction"[67] are what America uses as tools of foreign policy. Through the medium of the information environment, Osama bin Laden is directly engaging in information warfare in order to build negative consensus in the minds of the people of America and of the world in order to put pressure on key political decision makers. This event represents an asymmetric attack through the information environment to achieve strategic effects. When compared to how messages were transmitted in earlier eras of history (e.g. FM, AM, and short-wave radio during WW II), the impact of today's capability to reach and influence people through messaging is staggering.

Information-sharing technology has powerfully influenced the relationships between the components of the CT by connecting people from one nation to that of virtually every other

---

[65]Friedman, 8.

[66]Dru Sefton, *Bin Laden gives book new life,* The Seattle Times, Saturday, January 21, 2006 [document online]; available from http://seattletimes.nwsource.com, Internet accessed 5 February 2006. Used with permission from Dru Sefton, national correspondent for Newhouse News Service gained through e-mail correspondence with the author, 7 February 2006.

nation in the world. People, who are integral parts of a closed national system, are

simultaneously a part of a global community that vies for their ideological allegiance. Today's

growing global connectivity is becoming an increasingly powerful force within nations. A

government's ability to maintain the allegiance of its people during protracted conflict has

become more difficult because the passion of the people has become much more open to outside

influence. People have become the dominant component of the nature of war not only because

they can be influenced through the information environment but because they can actively and

responsively engage in an exchange of information and ideas. The ability to rapidly collaborate

and build the consensus needed to influence political decision makers exists with heretofore

unimaginable speed. US military doctrine already states that,

> Both governments and nonstate actors use propaganda to create awareness and influence
> opinion. Increased public access to information and the increased ability of various
> groups to manipulate the media challenge the authority of major institutions and may
> even threaten the sovereignty of some states.[68]

In the current war on terrorism, which is focused primarily against Al Qaeda and their

affiliates, one can see the difficulties the US faces in waging war against a non-state entity. The

above quote, while stated in doctrine and often espoused, has been much more difficult to

operationalize. Counterinsurgent warfare must first be defined as a battle of popular will. The

physical and nonphysical nature of a counterinsurgent fight is asymmetric. The government, or

the foreign government in the case of Iraq, is typically much superior to the insurgent force in

physical military might and capability. In the non-physical sense, the scales tip in favor of the

insurgent. The insurgent maintains a stronger natural position in terms of political will for several

reasons. First, "for the insurgent the war is 'total,' while for a foreign government it is

---

[67]Sefton.
[68]FM 3-07, 1-10.

necessarily 'limited.'"[69] Because the foreign government sees the war as a limited and possibly protracted conflict, fighting a total war is politically unfeasible as is fully mobilizing all of his resources.[70] Not only can the foreign power not mobilize fully for the war but the government must continually justify its position and actions in the war; the government must continue to sell or market the war in a way that sustains the popular will of its constituents – its people. Because of the inherent limitations imposed upon the foreign power "the guerrilla can win simply by not losing, whereas the counterinsurgent power can lose by not winning."[71] When the influence of global perception is added to this equation, especially when the counterinsurgent is trying to mitigate perceptions of his own unethical conduct, then the true challenge of counterinsurgent warfare in the Information Era begins to surface. Actions must consistently support stated values because a perception of legitimacy, and through it the popular will to support the war, must be maintained. Because perception and popular will are the key components of counterinsurgent warfare, they must be the first objective for planners at the strategic and operational levels. US Army doctrine has defined the information environment as a critical part of a commander's battle space, but actually planning and executing integrated information operations is often neglected.

In applying the effects of these technological advances to theories of warfare, Thomas Hammes argues that in Fourth Generation Warfare, an evolutionary form of Modern Warfare, "the fundamental precept is that superior political will, when properly employed, can defeat greater economic and military power."[72] Hammes' fundamental precept of 'superior political will' combines with what Friedman refers to as the 'leveling affect of globalism' to equal overnight perceptions that can threaten the counterinsurgent. Hammes explains that "operationally, it uses different messages for different audiences, all of which focus on breaking

---

[69]Andrew Mack, quoted by Jeffrey Record, *Why the Strong Lose,* Parameters, Winter 2005-06, 17.
[70]Record, 17.
[71]Record, 20.

an opponent's political will…and strategically…remains focused on changing the minds of decision makers."[73] The fundamental thrust of Fourth Generation Warfare combines with today's technological advancements in information flow and diffusion to equal the potential to affect the collective conscience of populations. Through the reporting of events that create perceptions of, or that highlight actual disconnects between, actions and values, a general consensus may be created that can influence strategic-level decision makers. Furthermore, these perceptions are compounding and prone to distortion.

An initial perception, created by the reporting of unethical actions, has a compounding nature because a series of additional assumptions are generated that will be biased depending upon the audience receiving the report. These additional assumptions, in turn, bring to mind new perceptions. Similarly, the initial perception can become distorted. Like the child's game *whisper-down-the-lane* where children in a circle secretly whisper a short phrase from one to another in order to laugh at how distorted that phrase becomes. In the same way, the final understanding of the initial action will also have become distorted by ever growing assumptions and perceptions. BG Vincent Brooks, the Army's Chief of Public Affairs, calls these growing and changing perceptions the 'ink-blot phenomenon.' The initial perception widens just like an ink-blot as it takes on more and more mutations making it very difficult to accurately understand the facts of the initial action. In all information events concerning unethical behavior on the part of the counterinsurgent, it is difficult to combat 'wrong' perceptions and relate the facts of what really happened. Furthermore, it is difficult for the counterinsurgent government to re-

---

[72]Thomas Hammes, *Insurgency: Modern Warfare Evolves into a Fourth Generation,* Strategic Forum, No. 214, January 2005 (Washington, DC: Institute for National Strategic Studies, 2005), 1.
        [73]Hammes, 1.

enfranchise the people by countering the negative event through the follow-up reporting of actions taken to correct the misperception and/or misconduct.[74]

Understanding that legitimacy is of utmost importance in counterinsurgent war is not a new concept. But, with the advent of the Information Era when a tactical-level action (i.e. an action that is considered an atrocity) is placed into the information environment, it can have an adverse strategic effect on the counterinsurgent much more quickly than in times past. In fact, even *alleged* unethical behavior can have adverse effects almost instantaneously. The Information Era represents an undeniably unique time in the history of warfare when the perception of an act reported one morning, whether accurately or not, can by the next morning disenfranchise the counterinsurgent from the population for whom he is fighting and from the population that sent him. While the flow of information may be manageable, the management of consequence is not.

The Tipping Point

Malcolm Gladwell wrote a bestselling book in 2000 called *The Tipping Point,* which explains how a combination of key elements can have powerful effects. In his online question-and-answer website, Mr. Gladwell states "that ideas and behavior and messages and products sometimes behave just like outbreaks of infectious disease. They are social epidemics."[75] His theory is that three phenomena work together to cause tipping points: contagious behavior; the fact that little causes can have big effects; and change happens not gradually but at one dramatic moment.[76] He also states that there are three types of people responsible for much of the change experienced in society: connectors, mavens, and salesmen. Connectors are people who seem to

---

[74]Brooks, Interview with the author, 12 January 2005.
[75]Malcolm Gladwell, *What is the Tipping Point About?* [Document online]; available from http://www.gladwell.com, Internet, accessed 7 February 2006.
[76]Malcolm Gladwell, *The Tipping Point* (Boston: Back Bay Books, 2002), 7-9.

know everyone; in a sense they collect people through what are called 'weak ties,' which are friendly yet casual acquaintances.[77] Mavens are people who accumulate knowledge. They are what we call 'subject matter experts' or 'go to' people in the military and are living data banks[78] of specific or general knowledge. Salesmen, according to Gladwell, are persuaders; uniquely charismatic people who seem to have answers to any objection against something they are trying to sell.[79] Tipping-point salesmen are so good at defeating any objections to what they are selling that they are almost always successful at persuading their targeted audience. When the *tipping point theory* is adapted to 21st century warfare, and especially counterinsurgent warfare, one finds all of its characteristics present in the components of the information environment.

The little causes that can have big effects are the unethical actions on the battlefield that are reported or captured in written, audio, or visual form. The contagious behavior is the ever-increasing sharing and networking of information. The dramatic change, or tipping point, comes when these things working together spark action in the physical world, as was seen all across France with the Muslim youth riots in November 2005. These incidents were reportedly sparked by the suspicious deaths of two Muslim youths electrocuted in a Paris electricity sub-station. The suspicious perception of this event acted as a tipping point within the Muslim community, a community that shared a collective identity as a Diaspora of Muslims within a globally networked Islamic society. It was the collective conscience of this community as a disenfranchised people, with the feeling that they were being maltreated by French society, and in a larger sense that they were at war with the West that fueled, grew, and sustained the riots and destruction well beyond the expectations of French authorities. This collective identity is enabled and fostered through globally networked information connectivity. When one looks for Gladwell's mavens, connectors and salespersons, they need look no further than the information environment.

---

[77]Gladwell, 46.
[78]Gladwell, 70.

Literally at one's fingertips are boundless data banks of information, accessible through powerful search engines (mavens), cell phones, e-mail, instant messaging, collaborative networks, blog sites, chat rooms, and forums (connectors). In the case of Al Qaeda and the war on terror, one has any number of salesmen from which to pick: Osama bin Laden, et al., as well as any number of other influential religious and political leaders.

Another example of the tipping point power of the information environment was seen after the September 2005 Danish newspaper release of a cartoon depicting the Prophet Muhammad wearing a turban in the form of a bomb. One would expect the cartoon of a locally distributed newspaper to deeply offend Muslims at the local level. Because of today's globally networked information environment, however, there have been protests and demonstrations across the Muslim world and throughout Europe that have continued up until the writing of this current study over seven months later. "Clerics in Palestinian areas called in Friday prayers for a boycott of Danish and European goods and the severing of diplomatic ties. Tens of thousands…marched through Palestinian cities, burning the Danish flag and calling for vengeance."[80] The cartoons were reprinted in over 20 other countries; Muslims sought a UN resolution against the Danish; protesters burned the Danish consulates in Beirut and Syria; and a protester was shot and killed in Laghman province Afghanistan.[81] The speed and intensity of these kinds of wide-spread reactions were extremely rare in times past. The power and influence that these kinds of information events trigger in the physical world must be considered in the counterinsurgent battlefield, especially where cultural and religious sensitivities prevail.

---

[79]Gladwell, 70.

[80]Jan Olsen, *Muslim outrage exposes deep rifts,* The Mercury News, 4 February 2006 [document online]; available from http://www.mercurynews.com/mld/mercurynews/news/13791415.htm, Internet, accessed 7 February 2006.

[81]Wikipedia, *Jyllands-Posten Muhammad cartoons controversy* [document online]; available from http://en.wikipedia.org/wiki/Jyllands-Posten_Muhammad_cartoons_controversy#_note-0 , Internet, accessed on 7 February 2006.

A New Reality in the Conduct of Warfare

Information must be seen as the heart of 21st Century Warfare. The information environment must be conceptualized similar to physical battle space and treated accordingly. As stated by Jeffrey Record in his article *Why the Strong Lose*, America has a "tendency to separate war and politics—to view military victory as an end in itself, ignoring war's function as an instrument of policy."[82] In other words, American military commanders are fixated on the kinetic fight and have forgotten the non-physical nature of war. This is an especially critical mistake to make in irregular, asymmetric warfare when the objective is building legitimacy and sustaining political will in order to win rather than destroying the enemy physically. American commanders in Iraq over the last two years have learned this lesson. MG Peter Chiarelli related this truth graphically in a Power Point™ briefing on how he dealt with insurgents in Sadr City in Iraq. As Figure 6 shows, MG Chiarelli came to understand that everything he did had to be nested in what he called 'Full Spectrum Information Operations.'

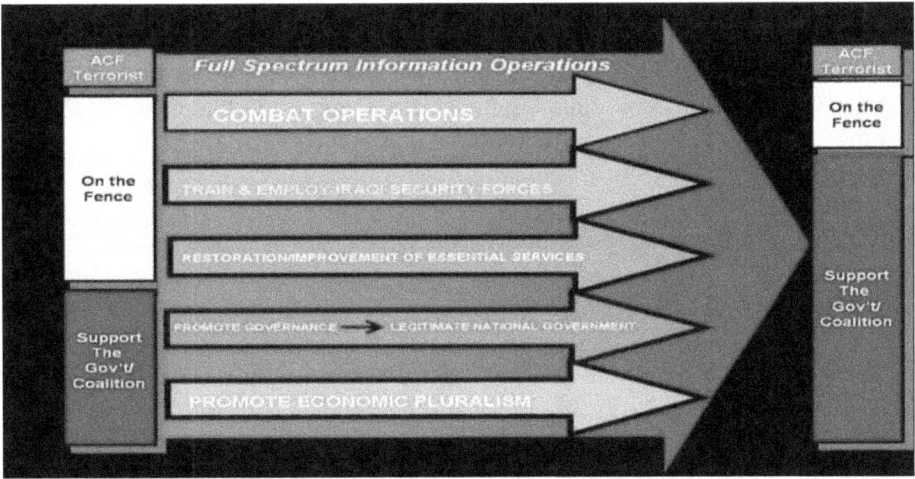

---

[82]Record, 24.

Figure 6. The Information Operations Line of Operation[83]

MG Chiarelli and others in Iraq are relearning what the Founding Father's took for

granted as common knowledge: when a people feel their basic rights are being violated, they

rebel. Everything the counterinsurgent does, therefore, must send the message that it is necessary

for the protection of those inalienable rights. Ted Gurr explained this as 'value expectations' and

said that when there is a perception of 'relative deprivation' of these "conditions of life to which

people believe they are rightfully entitled," conditions have been set for collective violence. [84]

An article that MG Chiarelli and Major Patrick Michaelis wrote for the *Military Review* related

that they had come to the realization that because of the power of the media and the speed of

information flow, their division's daily tactical operations were being played out not only locally

on the streets of Baghdad, but both nationally and internationally as well. They also articulated

that the first and all-encompassing planning consideration for all operations should be to

understand and plan operations from the perspective of the Iraqi people.[85] Specifically stated was

the new reality that,

> The actions of soldiers and leaders and their efforts on the ground can resonate at a
> strategic level in an instant. Shaping the message and tying that message to operations is
> as important, if not more so, to the desired individual effect as the previous five lines of
> operations.[86]

The challenge to the American military institution today is acting on the sentiments and

hard-learned lessons of MG Chiarelli and others. However, realizing what is necessary and doing

what is necessary are two different things. The US military's use of the information environment

---

[83]Peter Chiarelli, *Task Force Baghdad, Operation Iraq Freedom II,* from a Power Point™
Presentation briefed by MG Chiarelli, Commanding General, 1st Cavalry Division, to the Command and
General Staff Officer Course, 1 April 2005.
    [84]Ted Gurr, *Why Men Rebel* (Princeton, NJ: Princeton University Press, 1970), 13.
    [85]Peter Chiarelli and Patrick Michaelis, *Winning the Peace, The Requirement for Full-Spectrum
Operations,* Military Review, July-August 2005, 14-15.
    [86]Chiarelli and Michaelis, 14.

and information operations as a line of operation is sorely lacking at the operational and strategic levels. The military seems to have a serious aversion to the media, which is not entirely unjustifiable. The media industry has consistently shown that its bottom line is its priority, and that its bottom line is based on what sells: death, destruction, and the perception of corruption. The reporting practices of the media by and large have been extremely damaging to the perception of what the war-fighter has been trying to accomplish on the ground and, thus, damaging to both the popular will (people) and political will (government) of the United States. More specifically, the majority of the reporting has been focused on those events that actually serve to emphasize only the negative aspects of the counterinsurgency; time and again, the media has created the perception of disconnect between American actions and values. If the principle of legitimacy is as critical as the Joint Publication for Military Operations Other Than War (MOOTW) states… if "committed forces must sustain the legitimacy of the operation and of the host government" to create "a strong impulse to support the action"[87] then the US military planner must harness the incredibly fast moving dynamics of the information environment with a global vision. Planners must do this through all of the mediums of the information environment in a way that reflects ethical conduct that supports stated values, that is honest and transparent, and that will magnify the effects of combat actions on the ground. The people component of the CT has become too powerful not to consider. Furthermore, the people component no longer simply refers to the people of the counterinsurgent's nation, but to a globally networked series of nations and non-state people groups, such as the Muslim Diaspora.

---

[87]JP 3-07, 2-5.

CHAPTER 4: Unethical Information Events in the Industrial and Information Eras of War

Having established a theory of warfare for the 21st century, an evaluation of its application through historical analysis is necessary. In order to accomplish this, four information events have been selected: two from the Industrial Era and two from the Information Era of Warfare. Each of the events is related to counterinsurgent actions that have been identified as atrocities or unethical, inhumane behavior on the battlefield. The analysis of each of these events first begins with historical background in order to set the stage, followed by a recounting of the event itself. Secondly, how the information environment was used to create perceptions, and thirdly the overall effects of each event based upon: 1) changes that were made at the operational to tactical level within the theater of operations, and 2) lasting institutional changes in regards to military doctrine, foreign policy, or law. Technical differences in how events are type-classified, whether as atrocities or less egregious unethical actions, are not at issue in this analysis. The thrust of this analysis is determining how the perceptions of these events through the information environment affected the nature of the conflict with which they are associated.

The Water Cure

A form of torture known as the 'water-cure,' which was supposedly in widespread use by American soldiers during the Philippine War (1899-1902), is the first event of the Industrial Era to be considered. The US had purchased the Philippine Islands (PI) from Spain following its defeat in the Spanish-American War of 1898. By the time of the Spanish-American War, Filipinos had been fighting for their independence from Spain for three years; immediately following the war on 12 June 1898, the Filipinos declared their independence. Even as the US was sending troops to occupy the PI with plans to colonize it for America, Filipinos were exercising their new-found independence by declaring Emilio Aguinaldo as their new president, organizing a Filipino Congress, and drafting a constitution. At first, the Filipinos welcomed American military occupation of the PI because America was seen as an ally that had supported the Filipinos in their hard-won independence. After the occupation, however, tensions grew between the desires for Filipino independence and American colonization. Barely a month after Aguinaldo was declared president, these tensions escalated into war. On 4 February 1899, an American soldier shot a Filipino soldier, resulting in the initiation of hostilities and the Battle of Manila. Aguinaldo was immediately declared an outlaw bandit by the U.S. Over the next twelve months of fighting the American army slowly gained control over the capital city of Manila. The Philippine Army of Liberation was forced north within the main island of Luzon, whereupon Aguinaldo gave orders to initiate a guerrilla phase of the war. One Filipino defeat led to another, until finally US Army Captain Fredrick Funston caught Aguinaldo in his guerrilla command post using a clever ruse. He posed as a captive, and along with the help of Filipinos, who had joined the American side, gained entrance into Aguinaldo's camp. The deception enabled Funston to get close enough to initiate a surprise attack that overpowered Aguinaldo's guards, capturing him in the process. This daring exploit marked the beginning of the end of resistance within the PI. Aguinaldo's capture, however, initiated a series of actions by the guerrillas that would escalate the use of extreme counterinsurgent measures that included atrocities.

Reportedly, Americans used methods of torture that included, among other things, the water-cure. Brian Linn provides the most comprehensive look at US involvement in the Philippines in his book, *The Philippine War 1899-1902,* written in 2000. He relates that the most notorious method of torture was the water-cure. According to Linn, investigations of the use of the water-cure produced such contradictory reports, that reliable conclusions could not be made, even though its practice seems to have increased over the course of the war.[88] Linn recounts a

---

[88]Brian Linn, *The Philippine War, 1899-1902* (Lawrence, KS: University Press of Kansas, 2000), 223.

witness's description of the water torture, "The victim is laid flat on his back and held down by his tormentors. Then a bamboo tube is thrust into his mouth and some dirty water, the filthier the better, is poured down his unwilling throat."[89] Other eyewitness accounts include the use of a handful of salt pushed into the nose of the victim during the water-cure as a further coercive measure. This practice seemed to be widespread in its use because of the isolated disposition and size of the American units. Reports also indicate that most of the abuse was the result of "small groups of men under junior and non-commissioned officers searching for weapons and information."[90]

The information environment at the time consisted primarily of the use of telegraph wire to transmit stories reported by newspaper journalists. The source of some of the most telling reports were letters written home to loved ones. These letters often contained braggadocios accounts of actual atrocities that were being committed. Cartoons, such as the one carried in the *New York Journal* on 5 May 1902 (Figure 7), and captioned "KILL EVERY ONE OVER TEN,"[91] had a powerful effect on the public. The famous American writer and storyteller Mark Twain, among others, added to the outcry by forming an anti-war coalition that spoke out strongly against the war.

---

[89]Linn, 223.
[90]Linn, 222.
[91]Wikipedia, *Philippine-American War* [document online]; available from http://en.wikipedia.org/wiki/Philippines-American_War#Origins_of_the_War , Internet, accessed on 17 February 2006.

Photo Removed Due to Copyright Restrictions

Figure 7. The Power of the Press in the Industrial Age

While the direct effects of the journalistic writings of reporters and celebrities such as

Mark Twain brought the war in the Philippines to the public's awareness, public concerns had no

direct effect on how the US military conducted the war in the field. Linn reports that atrocities

increased rather than decreased as the war progressed, especially toward the end of the war as the

army relied on increasingly harsh punitive measures.[93] The issue of the use of the water-cure was

investigated extensively by a Senatorial body called the Lodge Committee from 31 January 1902

to 28 June 1902, and did not result in any adverse actions toward the men or officers responsible

or any immediate changes in military doctrine or law. The Lodge Committee heard over three

months of testimony and specifically regarded eyewitness testimony of the use of the water-cure.

---

[92]Wikipedia, *Philippine-American War.*

The Army in the field operated primarily under the authority of General Order (G.O.) 100, which was passed in 1863 during the Civil War. This order outlined a policy of carrot-and-stick actions which restricted armies in the field, emphasizing their responsibility to restore order, to protect private property and to treat non-combatant civilians with dignity and humanity. On the other hand, G.O. 100 gave the Army the authority to deal harshly with guerrilla-type organizations or anyone aiding them, even to the point of carrying out summary execution in extreme cases. Americans understood that winning the hearts and minds was important during the war in the Philippines. G.O.'s 1, 40, and 43 all dealt with winning the support of the population through civil-action projects aimed at gaining the merit and the good will of the people.

Four US Army General Officers and one Navy Admiral testified during the hearings and overwhelmingly denied most of the allegations brought against their respective services concerning the general conduct of the war. General Hughes, testifying on 11 March 1902, said that the water-cure was never practiced in his command, except once "by the Macabebe scouts, who had promised not to repeat it."[94] This statement when taken in context with all of the other eyewitness accounts of the water-cure gives the impression that General Hughes was either willfully ignorant or that he felt that the actions of his command were justified and that he was before the Senate to defend the military's actions rather than take responsibility for practices allowed in their units. Indeed, much of the dialogue between members of the Lodge Committee and the General Officers carried with it a tone of arrogant belligerence on the part of the military officers. *The New York Times* newspaper printed the entire discourse of the Lodge Committee's testimonies, presenting a much more thorough coverage than one would find in today's newspapers, yet the people of the United States at the turn of the 20th century did not have the benefit of immediate ground truth and had to rely on the newspaper reports and conclusions of the

---

[93]Linn, 327.

Senate written in them. While both members of the Senate and members of the military, such as the Army's Judge Advocate General, General Davis, spoke out strongly against unethical behavior in the conduct of the war, their attention was given primarily to the individuals responsible for the unethical actions rather than the military as an institution. While the increased information connectivity and reporting of this event caused the government to address the issue of unethical conduct in Haiti, the public had an inherent acceptance and trust of their government and military. The popular support of the people for the military and trust of the government were maintained and the perceptions created by the reporting of these acts as well as the reporting of the Congressional hearings did not cause enough public fury to disrupt and change or 'tip' that trust. Furthermore, throughout the course of the war in the Philippines, even after accusations about troop misconduct began to surface, there is no record of additional restrictive measures put on the army at large, despite the Senate investigations. On the contrary, even the most extreme cases of atrocities involving American officers tried by a military Courts Martial ended in acquittal.[95]

My Lai

Men who take up arms against one another in public war do not cease on this account to be moral human beings, responsible to one another and to God.[96]

Later in the Industrial Era, My Lai, within the context of the Vietnam War (1957-1975), stands in sharp contrast to the 'water-cure' incidents of the Philippine War over a half century

---

[94]Wikipedia, *Lodge Committee testimony from the New York Times,* March 12, 1902 [document online]; available from http://en.wikipedia.org/wiki , Internet, accessed on 9 February 2006.

[95]Ryoo Moo Bong, *No Gun Ri Incident: Implications for the U.S. Army,* Monograph (Ft. Leavenworth, KS: School of Advanced Military Studies, 2001), 15-16. This reference concerns the acquittal of Major Waller and the reprimand of General Smith for their actions in connection with the execution of eleven native guides as one of the responses to the massacre of US forces at Balangiga. Major Bong's Monograph also notes the lack of public outcry over the atrocities; conversely he notes that General Smith was received as a hero upon arrival in San Francisco in August 1902.

earlier. Between these two small wars, much had changed in the world and in the technological advances of the Industrial Era. World Wars I and II had come and gone; the United States was one of two world powers in the bi-polar tension of a nuclear Cold War. Almost every household in America had a television and a telephone that were capable of reaching around the world.

With the defeat and withdrawal of the French from its Indochina colony in 1954, the United States chose to support South Vietnam's newly appointed president, Ngo Dinh Diem. The United States' main concern was stemming the spread of communism that had already prevailed in China, North Korea and North Vietnam. In 1954, the U.S. committed the MAAG (Military Assistance Advisory Group) to rehabilitate the South Vietnamese Army and to establish a 50,000-man Civil Guard force. The efforts of the MAAG were timely because between 1957 and 1960, communist insurgents were able to establish control over much of the South Vietnamese countryside through the executions of an estimated 1,700 village chiefs and elders.[97] As America was drawn deeper into the war in support of the pro-Western government of South Vietnam, the decision was made by the United States to introduce conventional military combat units. By 1968, the number of U.S. troops committed to the conflict had grown to approximately 536,000.[98] US military strategy in the war was decidedly conventional. General William Westmoreland, Commander, USMACV (U.S. Military Assistance Command, Vietnam), adopted the tried and true strategy of 'find the enemy, fix the enemy, and annihilate the enemy with overwhelming military fire power.' This strategy inevitably lent itself to metrics, such as numbering the enemy

---

[96]Richard Hammer, *The Court Martial of Lt. Calley* (New York: Coward, McCann & Geoghegan, Inc., 1971), 8. Francis Lieber, in setting down the regulations for the conduct of Union soldiers in the Civil War.

[97]Sam Sarkesian, *Unconventional Conflicts in a new Security Era, Lessons form Malaya and Vietnam* (Westport, CT: Greenwood Press, 1993), 82.

[98]Boot, 298.

dead. According to Williamson Murray, My Lai was one result of the "score card" mentality of

American commanders who were overly focused on an enemy body-count.[99]

On 16 March 1968, Lt. Calley's platoon from Charlie Company, 11th Brigade of the

Americal Division massacred between 300 to 500 civilians, mostly old men, women and children

in the village of My Lai. USMACV covered up the massacre until it "exploded in the American

press,"[100] sparking a fire-storm of outrage that greatly fueled the powerful anti-war movement in

the United States. Already, due to the influence of new communications technologies, this event

in and of itself became bigger than the collective abuses of over two years of counterinsurgent

combat in the Philippines at the turn of the century. This single unethical action stood in stark

opposition to the lofty political ideals that proponents of the war had argued as the reasoning for

fighting in Vietnam in the first place. If Democracy stands for freedom, and above all the

inalienable right to life and liberty, then the taking of innocent life was not only unacceptable, but

completely opposite of the most fundamental of American values.

In contrast to the use of the water-cure, the My Lai atrocity is extreme. It occurred

during the course of more than a decade-long counterinsurgent war. For the first time in history

televised news broadcasts reporting on the war reached down into the homes of individual

Americans and their families. Another dynamic directly affecting the social fabric of American

life at the time was the draft, which Congress had to initiate in order to acquire the necessary

troop strength to fight an increasingly controversial war. Additionally, the United States was in a

period of social transition, a transition that was brought into vivid focus by a new connectivity

through television, media, and telephone that did not exist during the Philippine War. The

heightened awareness of the war through these technological advances combined with the anti-

authoritarian social upheaval of the 1960's profoundly influenced the political process that drove

---

[99]Parker, 358.

the decision to discontinue the war in Vietnam. The United States was being pulled apart at the socio-political seams as these powerful new dynamics affects the conduct of the Vietnam War. The new multi-media market place of ideas[101] created by television and radio dramatically challenged the state's capacity to shape and control public opinion. In Vietnam the political war of wills had been engaged, and the North Vietnamese understood that America's strategic center of gravity was not its mighty conventional military but the popular will of its people.

The case of My Lai is simply one of many events that took place in Vietnam that added to the issue of that war's legitimacy as it was being reported and argued in the new multi-media market place. While an analysis of My Lai in the context of how the Vietnam War was prosecuted is important, a much more powerful example of the influence of popular will on political decision making can be seen in the aftermath of Lt. Calley's Court Martial proceedings. Lt. Calley was found guilty by a military jury of six officers made up of five Majors and one Captain, all of whom were combat veterans. Opening comments by the prosecution recounted the eyewitness testimonies of six soldiers who watched or assisted in the killing and of six additional soldiers who saw the carnage afterwards. Lt. Calley was found guilty on three counts of premeditated murder of no less than twenty-two persons and one additional count of assault with intent to commit murder. The court martial was conducted professionally and efficiently, in the best tradition of the U.S. Army, and reached a verdict of 'guilty' through an excruciatingly detailed adherence to due process. The Court's Martial verdict was founded on Article 118 of the UCMJ—Murder, which reads: "Any person subject to this chapter who, without justification or excuse, unlawfully kills a human being, when he has a premeditated design to kill and is found

---

[100]Parker, 352.
[101]Gil Gerom, *How Democracies Lose Small Wars* (Cambridge, UK: Cambridge University Press, 2003), p. 22.

guilty by a Courts Martial, is subject to a maximum penalty of death or a mandatory minimum

penalty of imprisonment for life with eligibility for parole."[102]

After the Court Martial returned this sound verdict, the American public reacted in a very

surprising manner. Despite international outrage and the clear evidence of guilt, "a poll

conducted soon after the verdict showed that nearly 80 per cent of Americans bitterly opposed the

findings…that 20 percent didn't think that what Calley did at My Lai was a crime at all, and that

most of the rest thought he was a scapegoat."[103] The fact that the America people, as a nation,

reacted in such a way means that people were either seriously misinformed of the details of Lt.

Calley's actions or that there was a much deeper nerve being touched. As noted by Richard

Hammer in the following quote, the reaction of the nation was overwhelming and exhaustive:

> From the left, from the right, from the center came a deluge of telegrams, phone calls,
> letters, petitions, demands. They flooded the courthouse at Fort Benning, the offices of
> Congressmen and other public officials, newspapers and radio and television stations, the
> White House. By a margin of more than a hundred to one, they challenged the conviction
> and the sentence on one round or another. They demanded that Richard Milhous Nixon--
> the President sworn to uphold the law--take action.[104]

While the response of the American public seemed hard to believe in the face of the

overwhelming evidence of Calley's guilt, President Nixon's actions were extraordinary and

almost without precedence. Despite the President's statement in reference to the war in Vietnam

"that he would never deviate from the course of law and justice no matter how loud the cries and

demonstration in the streets,"[105] he did bend to the collective popular will of the nation

concerning Calley's verdict. President Nixon took matters into his own hands and initiated a

process that ended with Calley's freedom after only three and a half years of house arrest. Calley

---

[102]About U.S. Military, *Punitive Articles of the UCMJ, Article 118—Murder* [document online];
available from http://usmilitary.about.com/library/milinfo/mcm/bl118.htm, Internet, accessed 20 February
2006. This definition of Article 118 can also be found in the Manual for Court Martial, 2002, Chapter 4,
Paragraph 43.
[103]Hammer, 374.
[104]Hammer, 375.

was sentenced to life in prison on 31 March 1971; one day later the President ordered that he be released from the stockade and confined to his quarters while the President reviewed the court proceeding. Due to public pressure, the President blatantly second-guessed the Military Court's Martial proceedings by intervening in order to ensure that the judges had reached the right verdict, and to determine if he should reduce the sentence. Less than five months later, Calley's life sentence was reduced to 20 years in prison. Following this initial interference the Secretary of the Army approved a clemency action that commuted Calley's confinement to ten years, after which "President Nixon notified the Secretary that he had reviewed the case and determined he would take no further action in the matter."[106] On 11 February 1974, Calley petitioned the federal district court for *habeas corpus* which the court granted on 25 September 1974, along with his immediate release.

The course of events following the trial and conviction of William Calley for the My Lai massacre represents the awakening of the people component of the CT and their decisive interaction in matters of war. When a Commander in Chief makes a decision to intervene in what appears in all respects to be an open-and-shut case of a mass-murder atrocity in order to assuage the emotional, collective outcry of the people, one can argue that the dynamics of the interrelated nature of the CT has changed significantly. The scope of this study does not allow a deeper look into the reasons why such intervention occurred. The fact remains that the people intervened, almost overnight. Because of their intervention, the people's newly decisive relationship to the government and the army during the course of war must be analyzed. Furthermore, at least a strong correlative link can be demonstrated between the information environment and the actualization of the people.

---

[105]Hammer, 379.
[106]Wikipedia, *Willian Calley* [document online]; available from http://en.wikipedia.org , Internet, accessed on 18 February 2006.

In the sixty years between the war in the Philippines and the war in Vietnam, huge strides had been made in the ability to reach people with information. Not only were radio and telephone communications vastly superior to what existed around the turn of the century, but the impact of the images of war on television, as well as the images of atrocities, carried with them a new power, a power that would change the key relationships between armies in the field and the people they served back home forever. The people had gone, in a very short time, from depending upon the government to interpret and disseminate much of what happened on the battlefield to being inundated with reports and images that they were left to interpret themselves. Like most other technological revolutions, the communications advances in the Industrial Era were both a blessing and a curse. While the army was made acutely aware of the necessity to properly manage information and to ensure that their Public Affairs Office (PAO) was accurately and honestly reporting critical battlefield events, the upcoming technological advances about to be unleashed upon the world in the Information Era would create RMA challenges that war-fighters never dreamed of in the previous eras of warfare.

Abu Ghraib

From the atrocity at My Lai, one must fast forward thirty-five years to address the events that took place at the Abu Ghraib detention facility in Iraq. As foreshadowed in the previous chapter, the world had changed more in the last three decades than it had in the fifty previous years. If My Lai marked the awakening of the people component of the CT, then the Global War on Terrorism (GWOT) has shown it to be fully actualized as a much more decisive influence in the conduct of war than in any previous era. With the end of the Cold War, the dissolution of the Soviet Union, and the rise of the United States as the world's sole superpower, the dynamics affecting conflict forced a shift from conventional to unconventional warfare. September 11, 2001, was a clarion call, marking the ascendancy of this age-old form of warfare within the

Information Era. With the overwhelming dominance of the United States' military in every aspect of conventional war fighting, adversaries had no place to go except to the unconventional realm. Enabled by the connectivity available in this new worldwide information environment, non-state and transnational organizations, such as Al Qaeda, were able to organize through global collaborative networks. Al Qaeda could raise and transfer the necessary funds to equip, train, coordinate and then successfully execute the single most devastating attack ever perpetrated on U.S. soil. And they did this terrorist attack, which included the hi-jacking of four U.S. airline flights and the subsequent use of the aircraft as missiles to strike strategic targets within the United States. Three of the aircraft struck their intended targets, completely destroying both towers of the World Trade Center in New York City and partially destroying the Pentagon in Washington D.C. Due to the efforts of a handful of courageous passengers, the fourth aircraft crashed in a western Pennsylvania field before it could be used to strike another target, presumably the White House. Approximately 3,000 people were killed in the attacks, most of whom were civilians.

In a stunning counteroffensive, the United States successfully attacked first Afghanistan and then Iraq, destroying government, military, and terrorist entities within those countries and replacing them with indigenous, democratic forms of government. While the justification of America's second preemptive offensive into Iraq has been a heated point of debate and controversy, both the U.S. Congress and the UN Security Council explicitly or tacitly authorized President Bush to use military force. Of key importance to this study is the fact that UN Security Council's support was essential to such an attack. UNSCR 1441 offered Iraq a final opportunity to comply with disarmament obligations set out in ten separate resolutions since the first Gulf War in 1991 and represented part of the diplomatic reasoning used in justifying the invasion. While this study is not concerned with the geo-political argumentation for or against such an attack, the fact that the UN is an essential political body in the authorization of a sovereign nation's use of force is a critical supportive point.

The Abu Ghraib incidents and the Sassaman incident, the final information event analyzed in this study, occurred in the context of the second military offensive in Iraq. Just 21 days after an extremely successful offensive operation, coalition forces captured Baghdad and other key cities, toppling Saddam Hussein's Ba'athist regime. Following the extremely successful conventional phase of the war, a complex insurgent war commenced with separate factions of the former Ba'thist party and Islamic extremists. During subsequent military operations, the tactical-level unethical actions at Abu Ghraib took place. The isolated, unethical conduct of a group of Military Police (MP), Military Intelligence (MI), and civilian contractors at the Abu Ghraib prison was widely recognized by both government officials and the media as having a very serious adverse strategic affect on what the United States Government was trying to accomplish in Iraq.

These incidents included various forms of torture and prisoner abuse that included beatings, indecent and sexually embarrassing posturing, threats of electrocution, and the use of police dogs to injure and terrorize prisoners. Pictures taken of these acts by the perpetrators were anonymously turned over to military Criminal Investigation Division (CID) by a concerned soldier. Not confident that he would not get in trouble for bringing this information to light, this same soldier gave a copy of the information to two different news agencies. The images subsequently surfaced in the information environment to include media and internet sources. These incidents directly affected both the strategic center of gravity of the American public's will and support for the GWOT and the operational center of gravity of the Iraqi people, because they were repugnant to *both* American and Iraqi sensibilities and values. And while the official reports of the independent panel and the Pentagon noted that the MP and MI relationship at Abu

Ghraib represented an aberration when compared to situations at other detention centers,[107] the effects caused by the release of these actions into the information environment was extremely powerful.

> Those pictures, the first of which were broadcast on the CBS program 60 Minutes II in the spring of 2004 showed that **much had gone terribly wrong in Iraq**, but more than dismay, they inspired revulsion. Whatever they thought about the Bush administration's reasons for going to war, most Americans believed that Iraq and the world were better off without Saddam Hussein and his torturers. Now here was evidence that only a year later in Abu Ghraib, one of Saddam's cruelest prisons, **Americans**, too, were torturing Iraqi civilians (italics added for emphasis by the author).[108]

The italicized portions of the above quote from Craig Whitney's introduction to *The Abu Ghraib Investigations* illustrates how the amplification and distortion of facts can create a negative perception within American minds, and worse, within Muslim minds, that does not accurately depict reality. The use of the phrase "much had gone terribly wrong in Iraq," and the word "Americans," connotes general and collective condemnation[109] of Americans as a people, rather than specific condemnation of the individuals responsible for the unethical behavior. The fact that only a group of five or six persons at the tactical level were responsible for the Abu Ghraib abuses, and not *all Americans,* is irrelevant. The perception of disconnect between actions and values at the national level had been created with both operational-level and strategic-level affect. Even more dramatic are Whitney's use of the word 'atrocity' in his introduction and his comparison of Abu Ghraib to the My Lai incident.[110] While one may acknowledge the relationship between prisoner abuse and the murder of 300 to 500 civilians as unethical, there is an extreme difference between the two. The word atrocity was not attributed to Abu Ghraib by either the independent or the Pentagon investigators, and therefore Whitney's use of the term is a

---

[107]Steven Strasser, Ed. *The Abu Ghraib Investigations, The Official Reports of the Independent Panel and the Pentagon on the Shocking Prisoner Abuse in Iraq* (NY: Public Affairs, 2004), 84.

[108]Steven Strasser, Ed., VII-VIII.

[109]Vincent Brooks, personal interview with the author, Ft. Leavenworth, Kansas, November 28, 2005.

[110] Steven Strasser, Ed., VII-VIII.

perfect example of BG Brook's 'ink-blot' phenomena spoken of earlier. More importantly, the action that must be taken for the USG to re-enfranchise the people offended by these acts becomes an extremely difficult task. The U.S. military is an organization that is not geared toward winning the battle of perceptions in the information environment. The necessary, comprehensive, general-officer-level investigations took months to complete, but in the information environment 'comprehensive' and 'responsive' are competitive concepts.[111] Neither the immediate measures taken by the military to prevent further abuse or the disciplinary action taken against the perpetrators, carry anywhere near the impact of the initial reporting of the scandal. The media industry is not in the business of U.S. government or military public affairs. If government or military representatives do not immediately and transparently inform the people through the media of events like this, the suspicion always exists that the truth is not being told or that it is being partially covered up.

The second- and third-order affects of Abu Ghraib, when compared to the affects of similar and much more egregious events of the Industrial Era, are extremely significant. Specialist Charles Graner was found guilty of all charges related to this event and was sentenced to ten years in a federal prison. Staff Sergeant Ivan Frederick was also found guilty of his charges and was sentenced to eight years in prison, forfeiture of pay, a dishonorable discharge, and reduction to the rank of private. Lynndie England was convicted, was sentenced to three years in prison, and received a dishonorable discharge. Three additional soldiers were tried and found guilty, each receiving penalties of six months to a year of confinement. The commanding officer of the prison, BG Janis Karpinski, was reduced to the rank of colonel, effectively ending her military career. None of the accused was charged with murder. Other affects caused by this

---

[111] Brooks, April 5, 2006.

event were felt directly by the Bush administration. Twice in 2005, Secretary of Defense Donald Rumsfeld submitted an offer of resignation to the President because of the Abu Ghraib scandal.

Department of Defense (DOD) reaction to the Abu Ghraib incidents caused an avalanche of cascading policies and directives to be implemented in both Iraq and Afghanistan. A memorandum was published by the office of the Secretary of Defense and signed by Donald Rumsfeld following an over 100 page independent panel review of DOD Detention Operations, as well as multiple reports on U.S. treatment of prisoners in Iraq by the Congressional Research Center, to ensure effective implementation of the following:

- All Federal employees, civilian contractors, and OGAs engaged in the handling or interrogation of individuals detained by the DOD, must complete annual law of war training[112]

- Secretaries of the Military Departments, CDRs of COCOMS, and other DOD Components responsible for Federal employees or civilian contractors engaged in handling or interrogation of individuals detained by the DOD shall complete an annual report NLT 31 OCT on the fulfillment of the training[113]

- The Undersecretary of Defense for Acquisition, Technology and Logistics will establish procedures to ensure that each DOD contract for persons performing handling or interrogation duties be required to receive and document training regarding the international obligations and laws of the United States applicable to the detention of personnel[114]

The three directives paraphrased above were followed by an additional five directives given specifically to the Regional Combatant Commanders, and an additional page of directives requiring specific reporting responsibilities that are binding through December 31, 2007.[115] Following exhaustive top-down measures, both joint and international doctrine was developed and updated with Joint Publication 3-36, *Detainee Operations,* published on 27 September 2005, as well as the NATO AJP-2.5(A), *Captured Persons, Materiel and Documents,* written for the

---

[112]Donald Rumsfeld, *Memorandum for Secretaries of the Military Departments, Chairman of the Joint Chiefs of Staff, Under Secretaries of Defense, Commanders of the Combatant Commands, and Directors of the Defense Agencies,* Subject: FY 2005 National Defense Authorization Act Provisions Regarding Persons Detained by the Department of Defense, April 11, 2005, 1-1,1-2,2-1.

[113]Rumsfeld Memorandum, 1-1,1-2,2-1.

[114]Rumsfeld Memorandum, 1-1,1-2,2-1.

purpose of providing "guidance on the procedures for the handling, administration and interrogation of captured persons (CPERS)."[116]

At the operational level, joint manuals were printed for the area of operations, such as *Detainee Operations in the Global War on Terrorism, Multi-Service Tactics, Techniques, and Procedures (MTTP) Package* that included an implementation suspense of 30 January 2006. At the tactical level, the Multinational Corps Iraq produced *Detention Operations Do's and Don'ts Smart Cards.* The reporting of any breech in the law of war concerning these issues by members of the coalition or civilian contractors became critical information to be reported to commanders immediately upon its discovery. Other restrictions were placed upon coalition forces as to how long a suspected insurgent could be detained without proof of his or her involvement in the insurgency. Figure 8 shows how unethical acts affect the conduct of war once they have been reported in the information environment and are cycled back through policies and directives to the military.

---

[115]Rumsfeld Memorandum, 1-1,1-2,2-1.
[116]NATO AJP-2.5(A), *Captured Persons, Materiel and Documents* (2nd Study Draft, January 2005), 8.

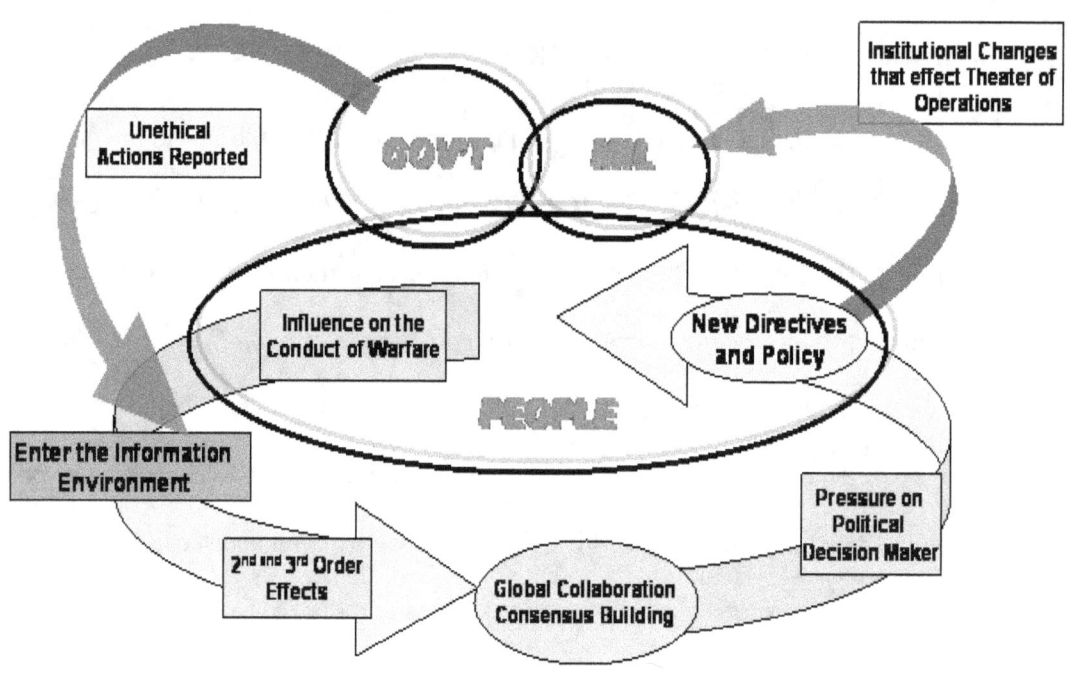

Figure 8. Driving the Nature of War in the Information Age

Once perceptions have been created in the information environment, they cannot easily

be countered. Perception management is one of the biggest concerns for the military, as

evidenced by the many institutional fixes implemented in response to these and other unethical

actions that are reported in the information environment. The US Army's PAO Chief is acutely

aware that the Army, as an institution is doing the right thing by punishing persons found guilty

of violations of the UCMJ. He is also aware of the immense amount of work that is being done to

correct unethical behavior: the investigations, research, doctrinal and policy reviews, and finally

the writing and implementation of command directives that enforce ethical conduct consistent

with the Army values at every level. Unfortunately, the PAO Chief is also painfully aware that

the US Army is not engaging in the information environment as well as it could.[117]   One of the

PAO's main missions is to inform people of what is being done to ensure Americans, and the

---

[117]Brooks Interview, 28 November 2005.

world, that we are acting in a way that embodies our most cherished values. We are definitely not engaging with the needed intensity to counter the negative perceptions of these unethical acts. The unfortunate fact is that 90 percent of the effort is expended to ensure actions are transparently reported to the public and to the world; therefore, in a sense, the effort is wasted because once an unethical act is reported the damage is done; mitigation of the perceptions created in the information environment are very difficult to counter. The bottom line up front is that we are losing the war of perceptions that is being fought in the information environment because we have not learned how to communicate through it as a battle-space. "That is, we have not collectively and institutionally learned how to create truth-based, timely effects that serve to inform the people and preserve freedom of action for the government while leaving the enemy weakened and vulnerable."[118] The war of perceptions, fueled by the relationship between actions and stated values, directly affects both political and popular will. Arguably, the war of perceptions should inform the physical war, as MG Chiarelli argues, at every level. In February of 2006, almost three years after the prisoner abuse scandal was uncovered and released to the public, new pictures of the event have surfaced. These new pictures were somewhat more graphic than the first and "threatened…to enflame public anger already running high over footage of British soldiers beating youths in southern Iraq."[119] Local Iraqis have separated themselves from the British in the area of the beatings and refuse to work with them. Figure 9 shows the impact unethical actions can have on the perception of reality. The picture drawn on the wall of the man with a black hood is a copy of one of the pictures released from the prisoner abuse scandal at Abu Ghraib.

---

[118]Brooks, April 5, 2006.

[119]Mideast.jpost.com, *New Abu Ghraib photos anger Iraqis,* Associated Press, [documents online]; available at http://www.jpost.com, Internet, accessed 21 February 2006.

Photo Removed Due to Copyright Restrictions

120

Figure 9. The Effect of Perceptions Created Through the Information Environment

This picture shows how images released in the information environment can make their way back to the street in a way that will seriously damage the image of the counterinsurgent. The message sends a very clear message with Lady Liberty pulling the switch that brings torture to the Iraqi. There is perhaps no better visual depiction that shows the disenfranchisement of the Iraqi people and a clear message of disconnect between American actions and American values.

Lieutenant Colonel Nate Sassaman

The story of what happened to Lieutenant Colonel (LTC) Nathan Sassaman and his mechanized infantry battalion in the Sunni Triangle of Iraq brings into sharp focus the juxtaposed

---

[120]Wikipedia, *Abu Ghraib Prison abuse* [document online]; available from http://en.wikipedia.org/wiki/Abu_Ghraib_torture_and_prisoner_abuse#Convictions_and_courts-martial ,

dynamics of warfare in the Information Era. On a personal level, his story is one of tested values; but within the context of a counterinsurgent war, it is a story of how important it is to understand the consequences of making decisions inconsistent with national values. LTC Sassaman embodied American religious values as the son of a Methodist preacher, demonstrated American cultural values as a star on the football field in high school and college, and inculcated American military values as a graduate of the United States Military Academy at West Point. Sassaman was a product of his environment, but had a strong sense of personal responsibility and self determination as he led his battalion in Iraq. These values were tested during that very difficult year.

Sassaman's overall approach to dealing with the insurgent problem in his area of responsibility in Iraq was one of heavy handedness that reflected the Cold-War mentality and culture of the US Army. He was exactly what the US Army wanted, expected, and, as far as institutional training allowed, had created. He was an aggressive and decisive combat leader. The problem was that LTC Sassaman was not fighting a conventional war, but an insurgent war. In insurgent warfare, the values that one thinks one truly believes become difficult to embody; values are tested daily by the ambiguity caused by the absence of a clearly identifiable enemy. As one *New York Times* journalist wrote concerning Sassaman, "[T]he straight lines and rigid hierarchy of the Army that had created him seemed, like so many other American ideas brought to this murky land, no longer particularly relevant."[121] In the incredibly complex environment of counterinsurgent warfare, and because of the aggressive, heavy handed command climate LTC Sassaman had set; men under his command disregarded the clear protocol that had been established for dealing with Iraqi citizens detained after curfew. Through the decisions of one of

---

Internet, accessed on 20 February 2006.
[121]Dexter Filkins, *The Fall of the Warrior King,* The New York Times. [document online]; available from http://www.nytimes.com/2005/10/23/magazine/23sassaman.html?ei=5089&rm=71v28g59c Internet, accessed on December 5, 2005, 1.

Sassaman's Platoon Leaders, Lieutenant Saville, these soldiers took matters into their own hands and decided to teach two Iraqi men caught out after curfew a lesson. Lt. Saville made the decision to force the two men to jump into the Tigris River to teach them a lesson, instead of following procedure and escorting them to the detention center. Whether intentional or unintentional, their methods reportedly led to the death of one of the two men. Following this incident, LTC Sassaman, one of America's most professional and outstanding combat leaders, made what is known as an irrevocable decision:

> [He] decided to flout his 19 years in the Army and his straight-and-narrow upbringing. He turned to one of his company commanders, Capt. Matthew Cunningham, and told him what to do. "Tell them about everything," Sassaman said, "except the water."[122]

His statement is a perfect example of tested values because within Sassaman's words one can see the contrast of right and wrong: "tell them about everything" presents complete truthfulness; "except the water" includes a lie of omission. Without enumerating the second- and third-order effects of this decision, one can guess the negative outcome. Crucial to the argument in this thesis is the premise that Sassaman's decision not to publicize what his men had done was based upon his reasoning that such publicity would incite anti-American feelings.[123] What he failed to grasp is that the issue of publicity was a moot point at the tactical level because in the close knit familial and tribal culture of Iraq news like this travels with lightening speed. At the operational level, this stellar commander was about to experience how unforgiving the environment and the institution of the Army had become. Strategically, LTC Sassaman's decision represented one of thousands that will collectively either make or break the war in Iraq by creating perceptions in the minds of the Iraqis they affect. Are Americans a *just* people who have the legitimate authority to wield power or are they people who simply have the power to compel coercion? JP 3-07, *Joint Doctrine for Military Operations Other Than War* states that:

---

[122] Filkins, 1.

[A]ll military personnel should understand the political objectives and the potential impact of inappropriate actions. Having an understanding of the political objective helps avoid actions that may have adverse political effects. In such operations, junior leaders commonly make decisions that have significant political implications.[124]

If this quote was not directly from a current Joint Publication, one could have argued that Karl Von Clausewitz had written it two hundred years ago. Understanding the political objectives that are related to the conduct of war, especially during counterinsurgent war, is crucial. Because of an intense loyalty to his men; a loyalty forged in the extreme situations of combat, LTC Sassaman lost sight of this and decided not to report the whole truth about what his men did on that fateful evening in Iraq. The outcome of his single decision resulted in the loss of a commander of over 500 men, the weakening of the army's operational hold on Balad and its surrounding area, and a potential information event that had to be dealt with immediately in order for it not to become a strategic perception nightmare. While this case did not turn out to be another Abu Ghraib, it did result in the Courts Martial of Staff Sergeant Perkins and Lt. Saville, who were both found guilty of assault and sentenced to six months and 45 days respectively. The battalion commander, LTC Sassaman; the battalion executive officer Major Gwinner; and the company commander, Captain Cunningham, were all given letters of reprimand by General Ordierno that included the words "wrongful, criminal and will not be tolerated"[125] that will most likely end their careers.

As in the case of Abu Ghraib, the damage done within the Iraqi community was most likely irreversible, especially with the loss of a family member within the close-knit Iraqi tribal society. While this incident certainly helped to disenfranchise the American counterinsurgent force from the Iraqi population in and around Balad, it also did much harm to the U.S. Army. One difference in this case versus the Abu Ghraib case is that an investigation into the incident

---

[123] Filkins, 13.
[124] FM 3-07, 1-16.
[125] Filkins, 15.

was quietly and quickly initiated. The implications of this event were not lost on the command as it became aware of the possibility of wrongdoing, and also of the affect the story could have, not on the Iraqis, but back home with the American public. It cannot be argued that punishment for unethical conduct under the UCMJ is not thorough; even in the midst of an extremely complex war the individuals responsible for this act were held responsible. But, as in the case with Abu Ghraib, thorough measures taken to enforce the law within our own ranks carries much less weight than the initial reporting of the wrong doing in the information environment. The Army lost four officers and one noncommissioned officer in the midst of an extremely difficult foreign, counterinsurgent war. These men were lost due to a single command decision that seemed acceptable in the context of the ambiguous counterinsurgent environment, but the fact remains, they were lost. They were casualties as real as if they had been shot.

CHAPTER 5: Conclusion -The Way Ahead

> Historical experience is written in iron and blood. We must point out that the guerrilla campaigns being waged in China today are a page in history that has not precedent. Their influence will not be confined solely to China in her present anti-Japanese war but will be world-wide.   -- Mao Tse Tung[126]

The thesis of this study is that when physical actions are not consistent with a government's stated values and are introduced into the information environment, they can be strategically adverse to the counterinsurgent. Stated another way, in the present information age, the age of globalization, it is very difficult for governments, especially foreign, democratic governments, to win counterinsurgent wars when the physical actions of their soldiers do not consistently support that government's stated values. What is the importance of the relationship between ethics and counterinsurgency? In a single word, the answer is *perception.*

Mao Tse Tung was correct in his prophetic statement that guerrilla campaigns would be worldwide. Guerrilla campaigns in the form of global jihad, being waged by transnational organizations like Al Qaeda, represent such a threat. Today's 'page in history' has been turned by the unprecedented communication and networking potential of the information environment. FM 3-07, *Stability Operations and Support Operations,* contains an excellent visual depiction of a drastically increasing operational tempo that can be shown to correlate with an increase in the speed of information with its fallout of global perception. Figure 1-4, entitled "Increasing Frequency of Operations," shows that over a forty-year period the United States Army was involved in eleven major operations, and contrasts that with the last fifteen years, which have yielded three times as many.[127] Although FM 3-07 calls these operations "unanticipated contingencies," among the examples depicted are the Korean and Vietnam Wars and the first

---

[126] Mao Tse Tung, *On Guerilla Warfare* [Document on-line.] at http://www.bellum.nu/literature/mao001.html, accessed 5 January 2006. 11-12.

[127] FM 3-07, 1-9.

80

Gulf War. The old state-on-state paradigm is still valid, but the added complexity of globally networked non-state actors who have shown the ability to inflict hugely disproportionate physical, political, and economic damage on existing states must be added. Instability in the world has increased. Since the end of the Cold War the capabilities of non-state entities have been felt in New York City, Washington DC, London, Spain, Jordan and the Ukraine, and have compelled the United States to wage a global war on terrorism.

"All military operations are information intensive…The cascading effects of events and their global magnification through the media further exacerbates this characteristic of the environment."[128] Military planners must see the news, media, and internet conglomerates as organizations that are biased to their own bottom line (whether economic, political or ideological), and planners must analyze these entities in such a way that maximizes their use in war-fighting. Planners need to study the information environment's systems at the national and global levels in order to understand each systems response and reporting cycle. The information environment is a crucial line of operation and therefore incorporating it into the planning and execution timetables at all levels of war is crucial. The objective of the DOD should be to maximize the use of the information environment through planned information releases of combat operations. More importantly, the DOD must release the information first. Jim Channon, writing about his concept of "The Millennium Force" in the 1970's after the Vietnam War, said teams "would drop into conflict areas and send out direct television coverage of the situation at hand."[129] While this author is not a proponent of Mr. Channon's full concept, the method he has conceptualized in his Millennium Force would be the kind of proactive use of the information environment that is essential in the Information Era.

---

[128] FM 3-07, 1-18.
[129] Jim Channon, The Millennium Force, Military applications in the global age, excerpt from a White Paper.

DOD planners must be prepared to deliver the immediate response that people demand and expect to receive through the media; in simple terms, the DOD must compete with the media. Operational-level planners and units must understand how to respond to the media by first knowing the media's purpose and mission at all levels, and secondly military planners must have a better understanding of their own purpose and mission based upon the law that gives them the authority to conduct war at all levels. When US troops are perceived to have acted unethically, when their actions do not seem to support their values, the event should be seen as an information opportunity, rather than an information disaster. Of crucial importance is the understanding that this is not a Public Affairs Office (PAO) issue, it is a command issue. The PAO cannot decide for a commander when he or she will engage through the information environment. If the DOD wants to succeed, entire organizations must think, plan, and act as communicators. The nature of the information environment, as a component of the battle-space in the Information Era of Warfare, demands it.

Planners must conduct a System of System Analysis (SoSA) to identify the full set of groups impacted by tactical, operational, and strategic actions. "The so-called 'war of ideas' cannot be a clever add-on to a military campaign. It must be at the center of the entire strategy."[130] In this increasingly globalized world, the numbers of different groups of stakeholders has grown much larger. These groups include international political bodies such as the UN; a much wider free-market system of interrelated businesses from the corporate down to the individual level; interconnected economic organizations like the European Union; and the old nation-state entities that still hold and wield the authority to use military force when compelled to do so. The complexity that unconventional warfare has taken on in the Information Era is staggering:

---

[130] Robert Leonhard, *The Evolution of Strategy in the Global War on Terror.* (Baltimore, MD: Johns Hopkins University Applied Physics Laboratory, 2005), 23.

Fourth-generation war, like its predecessors, will continue to evolve in ways that mirror global society as a whole. As the United States moves away from a hierarchical, industrial-based society to a networked, information-based society, its political, socioeconomic, and technological bases will also evolve...The key to providing for security lies in recognizing these changes for what they are.[131]

One entity that would help the U.S. compete in the information environment is a rival to existing media empires in the form of a government-run media agency at the national level.[132] If the key to winning counterinsurgent war is the popular will of the people, then we must engage that will through the information environment. Is this propaganda? No. The critical tenet that we must adhere to is the thesis of this paper: actions must support stated values. Therefore, information placed into the information environment must be brutally honest and transparent, especially when reporting unethical behavior by government or military personnel. Such reports must be reported simultaneously with detailed reporting of measures taken to correct the alleged unethical action. The government must address problems immediately and with utmost transparency, because the alternative is almost always damaging. If alleged unethical conduct is not immediately reported by the government and is placed into the information environment by any other agent, then the government already loses the perception battle, or at least starts from a much weakened position.

Al Qaeda represents a transnational insurgent organization that must be dealt with strategically, not only with direct kinetic means, but by discrediting its ideological underpinnings.[133] Al Qaeda and its affiliates are utilizing the information environment for all areas of organizational and operational sustainment. Especially true of the internet is its usefulness as a tool for building network linkages and fostering solidarity across borders. And, the uses of the written, audio, or visual forms of communication are extremely powerful tools in

---

[131] Hammes, 7.

[132] Ray Millen, quoted from a lecture to the School of Advanced Military Studies on Counterinsurgency, 26 January 2006.

[133] Michael Morris, *AL Qaeda as Insurgency.* Joint Force Quarterly, Issue Thirty-Nine, 42.

winning hearts and minds.[134] The use of the internet and technology to network is not a new concept. The U.S. Navy's Admiral Cebrowski was a leader in conceptualizing what has been called 'net-centric warfare' throughout the 1990's, with emphasis on electronic networks that combine the sensory networks of multiple platforms on land, on sea, and in the air in order to identify and destroy enemy nodes that would lead to the destruction of its system or network. Dr. Dorothy Denning at the Naval Postgraduate School is a leading researcher in the social aspects of the networking phenomena that has evolved since the inception of the World Wide Web. And, Dr. John Arquila partnering with other academics has adapted the concept of net-centric warfare to a new doctrine for war fighting called the swarming doctrine; he has also led research and development involving world-class computer hackers in order to uncover, track, and destroy adversarial computer networks. The United States has the tools and expertise to exploit the information environment from any technological or informational quarter. A huge reservoir of untapped talent lies in the corporate business world and in Hollywood. The USG and DOD must go out and recruit those with the expertise to know how to use the information environment better than anyone else: those within the movie and marketing industries. This kind of recruitment was commonplace during World War II; there is no reason it should not be the same for the Global War on Terrorism. Existing capabilities must be brought together in order to directly develop tools for effecting the information environment.

Similar to the new concept of the Intelligence Campaign Plan (ICP), which lays out in excruciating detail the apportionment of assets from a Combatant Command's plan down to its nested operational- and tactical-level plans, there must be an Information Environment Campaign Plan (IECP). The IECP should lay out in excruciating detail the information assets to be apportioned from the COCOM level on down. These plans should specifically address the

---

[134] Angel Rabasa, C. Benard, P. Chalk, C. Fair, T. Karasik, R. Lal, I. Lesser, & D. Thaler, *The Muslim World after 9/11* [document online]; available at www.rand.org, printed in PDF format as a part of

action-to-value message that must be sent through the information environment and should be intimately synchronized with all operational- and tactical-level actions on the ground. Optimally, maneuver and information plans would be structured in a way to maximize the speed and diffusion of information globally in a preemptive rather than reactive way, in a sense driving the information environment's reporting cycle. The ability to understand global information environment systems and processes would require an in depth analysis of globally networked communications, with an emphasis on understanding and exploiting the information-flow loop. That is, planners must understand the 'physical action to reporting' cycle, and how and when it can most powerfully affect the perspective of the target audience. Thomas Friedman in interviewing military planners at a theater command center in Qatar noted that:

> [T]his technology has "flattened" the military hierarchy – by giving so much information to the low-level officer, or even enlisted man, who was operating the computer, and empowering him to make decisions about the information he was gathering…the days when only senior officers had the big picture are over. The military playing field is being flattened.[135]

Mr. Freidman never made a truer statement and his comments are just as applicable to the enemy. Access to the information environment through all of the new and incredible technological advances have flattened the playing field, empowering individual members of transnational, non-state organizations to be disproportionately dangerous. The German's say, *"Nach dem Spiel ist vor dem Spiel!"* –After the game is before the game! One action leads to a perception created through the information environment, which influences the next action, which leads to a perception created though the information environment, and so on. The United States DOD must acknowledge the battlespace of the information environment and begin to attack the enemy through it with the attention to detail that it gives the physical environment, and only then can the US DOD decisively engage the enemy through this perpetual cycle.

Project Air Force, p. 470.

Understanding the relationship between ethics and counterinsurgency is critical because in the present Information Era perceptions created by actions, that do not support stated ethical values, can have strategic-level affect. Combinations of technological advances that comprise the information environment, and the inexpensive availability of the means to access that environment, have enabled the global networking of information, economics, and ideas on an unprecedented scale. Throughout history the people component of the Clausewitzian Trinity has gradually gained influence in correlation to its ability to receive information and communicate its desires to its government. Today, through the dynamic of the speed and diffusion of information, the people component of the CT is more influential than ever. Actions must support a governments stated values when that government has involved its military, and its citizenry, in counterinsurgent warfare, because a persistent perception of disconnect between actions and stated values will ultimately lead to a loss of popular support for that war. Just as one division commander noted shortly after his return from Iraq, "The enemy is using the internet; they are digitally connected, and the media is instantaneous," military planners must grapple with the fact that every action taken during combat can instantaneously become a perception issue in the information environment.

Finally, in a presentation to the 2006 class of the Command and General Staff College, Chief of Staff of the Army, General Peter Schoomaker stated words to the effect that despite the ambiguity of the counterinsurgent battlefield and the incredibly challenging transformation presently taking place in the Army, there was one thing that made the American soldier capable of moving in any direction and accomplishing any mission—the American values that he carries within himself. The US DOD must therefore win the perception war before it gets started; it must do this by teaching, emphasizing and enforcing those enduring American values enshrined in the

---

[135] Friedman, 39.

Declaration of Independence, the Constitution of the United States, and the writings of the Founding Fathers, like President George Washington's farewell address. In this way, through education followed by rigorous and realistic training, the DOD will guard against unethical behavior on the counterinsurgent battlefield and in doing so, simultaneously win the perception war along with the hearts and mind of the people.

APPENDIX

Use of the term *counterinsurgency* (COIN) is consistent with the DOD definition, "Those military, paramilitary, political, economic, psychological, and civic actions taken by a government to defeat insurgency."[136]

References to *Just-war* or *Jus ad bellum* are made with an understanding that to be a "just war," hostilities should only be initiated when the following criteria have been satisfied: 1) just cause: the protection and preservation of value; defense of the innocent against armed attack, retaking persons, property, or other values wrongly taken; 2) right authority: the person or body authorizing the use of force must be the duly authorized representative of a sovereign political entity; 3) right intention: the intent must be in accord with the just cause and not territorial aggrandizement, intimidation or coercion; 4) proportionality of ends: the overall good achieved by the use of force must be greater than the harm done; 5) last resort: determination at the time of the decision to employ force that no other means will achieve the justified ends sought; 6) reasonable hope of success: prudent calculations must be made to ensure a reasonable chance for success. *Jus in bello* refers to the use of force during war and states that there must be proportionality of means; means causing gratuitous violence or other unnecessary harm are to be avoided, and finally, protection/immunity must be granted to noncombatants.[137]

The Ethics Research Center (ERC) is an online resource that defines *ethics* with the following key components that have been adopted for this study: "(1) decision, choices, and actions that reflect *values*, (2) a set of standards of conduct based on *values* that guide decisions and actions, (3) a set of moral principles or *values*, and (4) a theory or system of moral *values* and

---

[136] Department of Defense. Joint Publication 1-02, *Dictionary of Military and Associated Terms* (Washington, DC: Government Printing Office, April 2001), 127.

[137] James Johnson, *Morality and Contemporary Warfare,* (Binghamton, NY: Vail-Ballou Press, 1999), 28-29.

or guiding philosophy [Italics added by author for emphasis]."[138] The word 'values' is italicized in each of the components of the definition of ethics as a commonality to each because central to this study is the focus on the linkage between values and actions. One is acting ethically if his actions reflect his values.

Atrocity is defined in this study as "savage, cruel, murderous acts committed against defenseless civilians or prisoners of war by a military force or by a political power."[139]

The Information Age (IA) is defined as "the period where movement of information became faster than physical movement, more narrowly applied to the very late 20th century (about 1991) and early 21st century."[140] A key component of the IA that is emphasized in this study is the World Wide Web and the inexpensive global connectivity to it through the use of cell-phones, palm-devices, collaborative networks, and search engines such as Google. Combinations of these technologies have made the internet the "ultimate place to accelerate the flow of relevant information."[141]

---

[138] Ethics Toolkit from the Ethics Research Center, *Ethics*. [document online]; available from http://www.ethics.org/glossary.html , Internet, accessed on September 14, 2005.

[139] Cathal J. Nolan, *Atrocity*. The Greenwood Encyclopedia of International Relations, Vol. 1. (CT: Greenwood Publishing, 2002), 106.

[140] Wikipedia, *Information Age*. [document online]; available from http://en.wikipedia.org Internet, accessed on November 11, 2005.

[141] Wikipedia, *Information Age*.

BIBLIOGRAPHY

Books

Aristotle. *Book V.*

Augustine, Saint. *City of God.* New York: Image Books, 1958.

Boot, Max. *The Savage Wars of Peace.* New York: Basic Books, 2002.

Calvin, John. *The Bondage and Liberation of the Will, A Defence of the Orthodox Doctrine of Human Choice against Pighius.* Eds. A.N.S. Lane, Trans. G.I. Davies. Grand Rapids, MI: Baker Books, 1996.

Carr, Caleb. *The Lessons of Terror, A History of Warfare Against Civilians: Why it Has Failed and Why it Will Fail Again.* New York: Random House, 2002.

Christopher, Paul. *The Ethics of War & Peace, An Introduction to Legal and Moral Issues.* Englewood Cliffs: Prentice-Hall, Inc., 1994.

Clausewitz, Carl. *On War.* Princeton: Princeton University Press, 1984.

Denning, Dorothy and Denning, P. *Internet Besieged, Countering Cyberspace Scofflaws.* Boston: Addison-Wesley Professional, 1997.

Friedman, Thomas. *The World is Flat.* New York, NY: Farrar, Straus and Giroux, 2005.

Gehring, Verna V. Ed. *War after September 11.* New York: Rowman & Littlefield Publishers, Inc., 2003.

Gerom, Gil. *How Democracies Lose Small Wars.* Cambridge, UK: Cambridge University Press, 2003.

Gladwell, Malcolm. *The Tipping Point.* Boston: Little, Brown, and Company, 2000.

Gurr, Ted. *Why Men Rebel.* Princeton, NJ: Princeton University Press, 1970.

Hammer, Richard. *The Court Martial of Lt. Calley.* New York: Coward, McCann & Geoghegan, Inc., 1971.

Haseler, Stephen. *The Varieties of Anti-Americanism, Reflex and Response.* Washington, DC: Ethics and Public Policy Center, 1985.

Holmes, Arthur, Ed. *War and Christian Ethics.* Grand Rapids: Baker Book House Company, 1975.

Holy Bible, *King James Version*

Inbar, Efraim, Ed. *Democracies and Small Wars.* Portland: Frank Cass, 2003.

Johnson, James. *Morality and Contemporary Warfare.* Binghamton, NY: Vail-Ballou Press, 1999.

Josephus. *The Complete Works.* Trans. William Whiston. Nashville: Thomas Nelson Publishers, 1998.

Kuiper, B. K. *The Church in History.* Grand Rapids, MI: Wm. B. Eerdmans Publishing Co., 1993.

Lefever, Ernest W. Ed. *Ethics and American Power*. Washington, DC: Ethics and Public Policy Center, 1985.

Leonard, Robert R. *The Principles of War in the Information Age*. Novato: Presidio Press Inc., 2000.

Linn, Brian. *The Philippine War, 1899-1902*. Lawrence, KS: University Press of Kansas, 2000.

Luther, Martin. *The Bondage of the Will*. Trans. J.I. Packer & O.R. Johnston. Grand Rapids, MI: Fleming H. Revell, 2003.

Manwaring, Max and Court Prisk. *McNair Papers, Number Eight, A Strategic View of Insurgencies: Insights from El Salvador*. Washington, DC: The Institute for National Strategic Studies, 1990.

McDermott, John J. *Turning Backward, The Erosion of Moral Sensibility*, The Alice McDermott Memorial Lecture in Applied Ethics, Number Eight. Colorado: United States Air Force Academy, 1998.

Mileham, Patrick and Willet, L., Eds. *Military Ethics for the Expeditionary Era*. London: The Royal Institute of International Affairs, 2002.

Moral Obligation and the Military, Collected Essays. Washington, DC: National Defense University Press, 1988.

Nelson, Candice J., D. Dulio, and S. Medvic. *Shades of Gray, Perspectives on Campaign Ethics*. Washington, DC: Brookings institution Press, 2002.

Nolan, Cathal J. *Atrocity*. The Greenwood Encyclopedia of International Relations, Vol. 1., CT: Greenwood Publishing, 2002.

Robinson, Piers. *The CNN Effect: The Myth of News, Foreign Policy and Intervention*. New York: Routledge, 2002.

Parker, Geoffrey, Ed. *Cambridge Illustrated History, Warfare*. Cambridge, UK: Cambridge University Press, 2004.

Peters, Ralph. *Fighting for the Future, Will America Triumph?* Mechanicsburg, PA: Stackpole Books, 2001.

Pratkanis, Anthony and E. Aronson. *Age of Propaganda, The Everyday Use and Abuse of Persuasion*. New York: W.H. Freeman and Co., 2001.

Sarkesian, Sam. *Unconventional Conflicts in a New Security Era, Lessons from Malaya and Vietnam*. Westport: Greenwood Press, 1993.

Schaeffer, Francis A. *How Should We Then Live? The Rise and Decline of Western Thought and Culture*. Wheaton, Illinois: Crossway Books, 1983.

Strasser, Steven, Ed. *The Abu Ghraib Investigations*. New York: Public Affairs, 2004.

Townsend, Charles, Ed. *Modern War*. London: Oxford University Press, 1997.

Turabian, Kate L. *A Manual for Writers of Term Papers, Theses, and Dissertations*. 6th ed. Chicago: University of Chicago Press, 1996.

Tzu, Sun. *The Art of War*. London: Oxford University Press, 1971.

Van Creveld, Martin. *The Rise and Decline of the State*. Cambridge, UK: Cambridge University Press, 2002.

Walter, Barbara F. and J. Snyder, Eds. *Civil Wars, Insecurity, and Intervention.* New York: Columbia University Press, 1999.

Warry, John. *Warfare in the Classic World.* New York: Barnes & Noble Books, 2000.

US Government and Department of Defense Documents and Publications

Basilici, Steven and Simmons, J. *Transformation, A Bold Case for Unconventional Warfare.* Thesis, Naval Postgraduate School, Monterey, CA: 2004.

Bong, Ryoo Moo. *No Gun Ri Incident: Implications for the U.S. Army.* Monograph, Ft. Leavenworth, KS: School of Advanced Military Studies, 2001.

Department of the Army. *FM 3-07, Stability Operations and Support Operations.* Washington, DC: Department of the Army, 2003.

Department of Defense. Joint Publication 1-02, *Dictionary of Military and Associated Terms.* Washington, DC: Government Printing Office, April 2001.

National Security Strategy of the United States of America. Washington, DC: The White House, 2002.

NATO AJP-2.5(A). *Captured Persons, Materiel and Documents.* 2nd Study Draft, January 2005.

Rumsfeld, Donald. *Memorandum, FY 2005 National Defense Authorization Act Provisions Regarding Persons Detained by the Department of Defense*, April 11, 2005

Washington, George. *General Orders.* (Fredericksburg: 1778).

Declaration of Independence of the United States of America, 1776.

Articles

Biddle, Stephen. "Afghanistan and the Future of Warfare: Implications for the Army and Defense Policy." *Foreign Affairs*, November, 2002.

Channon, Jim. "The Millennium Force, Military applications in the global age." Excerpt from a White Paper.

Chiarelli, Peter and Michaelis, P. "Winning the Peace, The Requirement for Full-Spectrum Operations." *Military Review*, July-August 2005.

Hammes, Thomas. "Insurgency: Modern Warfare Evolves into a Fourth Generation." *Strategic Forum*, No. 214, January 2005, Washington, DC: Institute for National Strategic Studies, 2005.

Leonhard, Robert. "The Evolution of Strategy in the Global War on Terror." Baltimore, MD: Johns Hopkins University Applied Physics Laboratory, 2005.

Littman, David. "Human Rights and Creeping Islamism at the United Nations," lecture notes for the Advanced Operational Arts Studies Fellowship, The School of Advanced Military Studies, 6 October 2005.

Mack, Andrew. "Why the Strong Lose," quoted by Jeffrey Record. *Parameters*, Winter 2005-06.

Millen, Ray. "Counterinsurgency lecture," Ft. Leavenworth, KS: School of Advanced Military Studies, 26 January 2006.

Morris, Michael. "AL Qaeda as Insurgency." *Joint Force Quarterly*, Issue Thirty-Nine, 2005.

Rabasa, Angel, Et al., "The Muslim World after 9/11" [document online]; available at www.rand.org, Project Air Force

Electronic Sources

Ethics. Ethics Toolkit, Ethics Research Center. [document online]; available from http://www.ethics.org/glossary.html, Internet, accessed on September 14, 2005.

Filkins, Dexter. *The Fall of the Warrior King,* The New York Times. [document online]; available from http://www.nytimes.com/2005/10/23/magazine/, Internet, accessed on December 5, 2005

Gladwell, Malcolm. *What is the Tipping Point About?* [Document online]; available from http://www.gladwell.com, Internet, accessed 7 February 2006.

McDowell, Stephen. *The Bible, Slavery, and America's Founders* [document online]; available from http://www.wallbuilders.com, Internet, accessed 30 January 2006.

Mangi, Naween. *Pakistan: Better Late Than Never in Outsourcing.* Business Week online, 9 May 2005 [document online]; available from http://www.businessweek.com, Internet, accessed 11 February 2006.

New Abu Ghraib photos anger Iraqis. Mideast.jpost.com, Associated Press, [documents online]; available at http://www.jpost.com, Internet, accessed 21 February 2006.

Olsen, Jan. *Muslim outrage exposes deep rifts,* The Mercury News, 4 February 2006 [document online]; available from http://www.mercurynews.com, Internet, accessed 7 February 2006.

Organization of Islamic Conference Member States, The. Infoplease. [document online]; available from http://www.infoplease.coml, Internet, accessed 27 February 2006.

Provincial Reconstruction Teams (PRTs). Global Security.org. [document online]; available from http://www.globalsecurity.org, Internet accessed 17 February, 2006.

Punitive Articles of the UCMJ, Article 118—Murder. About US Military [document online]; available from http://usmilitary.about.com, Internet, accessed 20 February 2006.

Universal Declaration of Human Rights, *Preamble.* available from http://www.unhchr.ch/udhr/lang/eng.pdf, Internet, accessed 18 January 2006.

Sefton, Dru. *Bin Laden gives book new life.* The Seattle Times, Saturday, January 21, 2006 [document online]; available from http://seattletimes.nwsource.com, Internet accessed 5 February 2006.

Sheehan, Kim and Hoy, M. *Using E-mail To Survey Internet Users In The United States: Methodology And Assessment,* Journal of Computer-Mediated Communication, Vol. 4, Issue 3, March 1999 [document online]; available from http://jcme.indiana.edu, Internet accessed 5 February 2006.

Tse Tung, Mao. *On Guerilla Warfare.* [Document on-line.] at http://www.bellum.nu/literature/mao001.html, accessed 5 January 2006.

Wikipedia, *Abu Ghraib Prison abuse* [document online]; available from
http://en.wikipedia.org/wiki/Abu_Ghraib_torture_and_prisoner_abuse#Convictions_and_
courts-martial, Internet, accessed on 20 February 2006.

_____, *Cusus publicu* [document online]; available from
http://en.wikipedia.org/wiki/Cursus_publicus, Internet, accessed on January 24, 2006.

_____, *History of Warfare* [document online]; available from
http://en.wikipedia.org/wiki/History_of_warfare, Internet, accessed on January 9, 2006.

_____, *Homing pigeon* [document online]; available from
http://en.wikipedia.org/wiki/Homing_pigeon#History, Internet, accessed on January 24,
2006.

_____, *Information Age.* [document online]; available from
http://en.wikipedia.org/wiki/Information_Age#The_Internet, Internet, accessed on
November 11, 2005.

_____, *Jyllands-Posten Muhammad cartoons controversy* [document online]; available from
http://en.wikipedia.org/wiki/Jyllands-Posten_Muhammad_cartoons_controversy#_note-0,
Internet, accessed on 7 February 2006.

_____, *Lodge Committee testimony from the New York Times,* March 12, 1902 [document
online]; available from
http://en.wikipedia.org/wiki/Lodge_Committee_testimony_from_the_New_York_Times,
Internet, accessed on 9 February 2006.

_____, *Mail* [document online]; available from http://en.wikipedia.org/wiki/Mail, Internet,
accessed on January 24, 2006.

_____, *Medieval warfare* [document online]; available from
http://en.wikipedia.org/wiki/Medieval_warfare, Internet, accessed on January 28, 2006.

_____, *Philippine-American War* [document online]; available from
http://en.wikipedia.org/wiki/Philippines-American_War#Origins_of_the_War, Internet,
accessed on 17 February 2006.

_____, *Teleology.* [document online]; available from http://en.wikipedia.org/wiki/Teleology,
Internet, accessed on January 9, 2006.

_____, *United Nations* [document online]; available from
http://en.wikipedia.org/wiki/United_Nations, Internet, accessed on February 15, 2006.

_____, *Universal Declaration of Human Rights* [document online]; available from
http://en.wikipedia.org/wiki/Declaration_of_human_rights, Internet, accessed on
February 15, 2006.

_____, *Willian Calley* [document online]; available from
http://en.wikipedia.org/wiki/William_Calley, Internet, accessed on 18 February 2006.

Interviews and Lectures

Brooks, Vincent. Interview by author, November 18, 2005, Ft. Leavenworth, Kansas.

_____. Interview by author, February 12, 2006, Ft. Leavenworth, Kansas.

_____. Interview by author, April 5, 2006, Ft. Leavenworth, Kansas.

Chiarelli, Peter. *Task Force Baghdad, Operation Iraq Freedom II.* Leavenworth, KS: Command and General Staff Officer Course, 1 April 2005.

Passage, David. Interview by author, November 30, 2005, Ft. Leavenworth, Kansas.

www.ingramcontent.com/pod-product-compliance
Lightning Source LLC
Chambersburg PA
CBHW080312290526
45790CB00005B/2014